AF271374

HS413

BATTLE AT BEST

BATTLE AT BEST

by

S. L. A. MARSHALL

With a foreword by J. F. C. Fuller
Illustrated by Garver Miller

NASHVILLE

Copyright © S.L.A. Marshall
Copyright © Marine Corps Association
Battery Classics is an imprint of The Battery Press
P.O. Box 3107
Uptown Station
Nashville, TN 37219
ISBN: 0-89839-115-6

Printed in the United States of America.

Contents

To my great and good friends, two wise men in the art of warfare, J. F. C. Fuller and B. H. Liddell Hart, who have helped me immeasurably through the years.

Foreword

THIS is a book on war in the raw—war at its cutting-edge. As a human creature man is rational and emotional. But at the cutting-edge he is animal, framed in a struggle for existence. His and his opponent's life are at stake, and in the clinch both are hurled back into the jungle age of history, in which survival values replace peacetime moralities. Everything that helps the soldier to survive is good; everything that does not is evil.

Thus it has always been in war, and there is no getting away from it. For although a battle is a compound of many ingredients, without a cutting-edge it is no battle at all. Only when and where men meet, struggle and kill is the testing-ground of all strategy and tactics.

It is to S. L. A. Marshall's outstanding credit that he has sensed this more profoundly than other present-day military historians. While they within their own ambits rightly enough deal with all phases which go to make up a battle as a whole, his task is to concentrate his reader's attention on its final phase—how men feel and act in the presence of imminent death.

"My argument was," he writes, "that if we did not know how our men performed in battle, all the rest of it would be superficial. The test of America at war lay in the effectiveness of the hands on the combat line and not in how various headquarters interpreted what they were doing."

In brief, you may interpret what it feels like to have a bayonet thrust at your throat, but it can be no other than an hypothesis unless you have actually experienced it.

Again and again he drives this difference home. "Those who would understand the true nature of war," he says, "must begin by understanding man's own nature, in its strength and in its weakness and in that fine balancing of good and evil, compassion amid brutality, hope amid ruins, and laughter in the middle of death, which give man his unique capacity for survival."

Unlike the normal military historian, he does not sit in his study and consult documents and books. Nor does he visit field headquarters and pore over plans and orders. Instead he goes to the front, to the cutting-edge itself, to question the men who did the fighting and, when feasible, those actually engaged in it. This is a supremely realistic task, a plumbing of events while they are red hot.

Frequently, he says, he has found that "men under the strain of battle forget what they have said or done." As frequently, the discrepancies between their statements appear to be irreconcilable.

When that is the case, his procedure in unraveling the tangle is first to get hold of its loose end, to begin at the beginning and ascertain how the men in question were placed and what orders they were given at the start, and then from that lead, step by step, get each of them to tell him what he had done. Of one of these detective hunts—typical of many others—he says: "What came forth was not unlike the story of the fool for luck who falls in a sewer and comes up with a diamond ring . . . by the end we knew everything that had happened in this platoon despite the confusion of the night."

The reconstruction of the landing of the first wave at Omaha Beach is one of the great epics of World War II: "Merely to stay alive" was "a full-time job" in it; nothing counted but "the force of a strong example." As one participant said of another: "We saw no sign of fear in him. Watching him made men of us. Marching or fighting, he was leading. We followed him because there was nothing else to do"—words which deserve to be inscribed in letters of gold.

Essentially a battle historian, Marshall's war books are written to the crack of bullets and the thunder of the guns, and frequently his personal experiences are as instructive as the events he describes. For instance, of an occasion in the Korean War he writes:

"I took off afoot across the stretch with not another person in sight. Halfway, three mortar shells came in, exploding within fifty or so yards of me. The terror I knew was almost overwhelming. I ran until I was exhausted. It always happens that way. Be a man ever so accustomed to fire, experiencing it when he is alone and unobserved produces shock that is indescribable."

Over two hundred years ago old Marshal Saxe said: "The human heart is the starting-point in all matters pertaining to war." These words would make an apt motto on the title page of this book, which not only makes exciting reading, at times brutal and terrifying, at others heroic and sublime, but also fills a gap in military-historiography. I warrant that no one who reads it will lay it down without feeling that he himself has been in the combat line.

J. F. C. FULLER

BATTLE AT BEST

The Abashed Patrol

WE got together in a Dutch hay barn which was the quietest spot in sight and lay within the regimental sector. In addition to the surviving members of the platoon which I write about, the only other person present except myself was that scintillating soldier, Pat Cassidy, who was then the battalion commander and is now a General Officer. We had become close friends in Normany out of the Carentan action and it was because of that bond between us that I immediately took over the interrogation at Pat's request and he listened silently while I worked his men over.

For that was what it amounted to. Up until that time the battalion headquarters and higher authority had been unable to determine what had happened to Lieutenant Edward L. Wierzbowski's platoon during the days when the Battle at Best flamed ever higher. American soldiers can become extremely close-mouthed about any action which they fight in isolation, with no outside eye witnesses present, and this group had chosen to keep their lips buttoned for reasons which the command could not understand. Previous interrogations had gotten nowhere. The men told conflicting stories, when they talked at all, and for the most part they simply responded to questions in monosyllables.

Their manner this day as they sat before me in the hay was taciturn and dour. They did not even talk to one another prior to the beginning of the critique. Always before when I had noted this attitude in American GI's, it was because something reprehensible had taken place during their operation and they were loath to divulge it. I suspected that this was what we were up against, and I imagine Cassidy did too, though we had not previously discussed it. This is the reason why from the beginning I felt that I had to be rough.

As is the custom in such proceedings, I told Wierzbowski to stand up and tell what orders he gave and what he did thereafter which resulted in the platoon becoming engaged. The Lieutenant got away to a bad start. He was vague about his orders. He backtracked numerous times and when I tried to pin him down with direct questions, his answers were either evasive or unresponsive.

This went on for ten minutes which was long enough. It was time to pretend an anger which I did not feel. I said to him: "Wierzbowski, do you really think you can fool me? If so, you're just kidding yourself; I've been around too long. You're telling a pack of damn lies. I don't know why you're telling them but we will get to that in time. I'm certain that what you're giving me is bunk. No platoon ever engages in the way you have described and no officer who brings men through an action like this one ever performs as hesitantly. Now I want you to sit down because I've heard enough from you for the time being. Among your men here there must be at least one who has a clearer idea of what happened than you seem to have."

Looking somewhat stunned, Wierzbowski got back in the hay.

There arose a soldier wearing first class private chevrons but when he introduced himself he said: "Sir, I am Sergeant Hoyle."

Cassidy turned to me and said: "We just bumped him up from private to sergeant today."

Hoyle then continued: "Sir, the Lieutenant isn't telling the truth but he is not trying to deceive you for any good reason. Lieutenant Wierzbowski is sort of ashamed of us because some of his men at the end were captured, though they later broke away under their own steam. I think the Lieutenant is wrong about this whole matter. I believe that from beginning to end everything we did reflected great credit upon the United States Army. I intend to tell the truth about our action from here on out and I hope that the Lieutenant and the others will be as frank with you as I intend to be."

I turned to Wierzbowski and said: "Is Hoyle reading your mind?"

He replied: "Yes, sir! That's the explanation."

I said: "All right then, let's cut out the nonsense and get going."

But for this happening in the way it did, a story of almost incredible heroism would have been lost to the United States and Private Mann would never have received the Congressional Medal posthumously. There had been no citation for him up until that time, though today he is a living legend in Holland and thousands of little Dutch children annually make pilgrimages to the monument raised by the Netherlands in his memory. Mann, to the people of that country, symbolizes all that is best in the American character. But Mann was only one of many valorous Americans on that field. I would suggest that any one reading of these deeds must feel strongly that Wierzbowski and every one of his surviving men were worthy of the highest decoration, though only Mann was cited for extraordinary honor. Further I doubt that any operation in American annals was fought out more bravely than the Battle at Best and I certainly know of none in the ETO in which the fighting performance of Americans as a whole was more dauntless.

One other prefatory note is necessary. The story begins with two German generals in conversation. What they talked about, and in particular the timing of their remarks to one another, is related to the battle story in such bizarre and coincidental fashion that the incident may sound too good to be true.

In the months which followed VE Day, many of the German higher commanders became my prisoners, so that we together could organize their story of the higher conduct of the war. They lived at our headquarters in St.-Germaine and they dined at my officers' mess. The war was over and I saw no object in denying them such creature comforts as might be afforded. Among them was General Von Gersdorff, a lank cavalryman with a high sense of humor and a generally attractive personality. Gersdorff spoke excellent English and I believe in later years he migrated to the United States. One day at lunch in St.-Germaine we got into discussion about Operation Market-Garden and his contribution to this narrative came forth. I wrote down the direct quotations and filed them away for future use.

Battle at Best

MAJOR General Rudolph Christopher Freiherr Von Gersdorff, Chief of Staff of the Seventh German Army, sat at lunch with his friend, Colonel General Kurt Student, who had organized and commanded the German airborne forces.

It was a warm summer day and the meal was being served them on the front porch of the comfortable Dutch manor house which Student had taken for his temporary headquarters. Their conversations turned toward the reasons why the fortunes of the Wehrmacht seemed to be consistently declining.

"For one thing," said Student, "we have never learned how to mount an airborne operation."

"Fantastic!" said Von Gersdorff. "All that the others know they have learned from us. Look at Crete! Look at Eban Emael!"

"Yes, look at them," replied Student. "We make small successful experiments and then we stop. I am speaking about the real thing."

"And what," asked Von Gersdorff, "is the real thing?"

Before his companion could reply, the attention of both men was drawn to the southward. There was a dull but steadily mounting roar from out of the sky in that direction. The small cloud on the horizon, at first no larger than the hand of a man, seemed to spread and thicken as it raced toward them. Almost over them it broke—hundreds of Allied planes raining thousands of American paratroopers.

As they started toward earth in a drop as beautifully timed and regulated as the skill of man could make possible, Student stepped onto the front lawn and raised his hands skyward in a sweeping gesture such as a cheerleader makes when he wants attention.

"This," said Student, turning toward his companion, "is what I was speaking about—the real thing."

The scene was at Veghel, Holland. The day was 17 September 1944. Student was looking at the American airborne portion of Operation Market-Garden, that first Allied attempt to make a sneak crossing of the Rhine and enter into the flat and relatively unfortified plain of Western Germany.

Some few miles to the south of where Student and Von Gersdorff had to depart their table without waiting for dessert, the 502nd Parachute Infantry Regiment came to earth and assembled neatly and without untoward incident in several flat fields just north of the Wilhelmina Canal.

It had initially, and according to plan, the least spectacular assignment in the whole show. The 101st Division's general assignment was to seize and hold the southern third of the attenuated corridor over which British XXX Corps hoped to roll from the Belgian border to the north bank of the Rhine. With the Guards Armored leading, XXX Corps expected to roll up this airborne carpet and consolidate the hold on Arnhem within fifty-six hours.

That this was not done finally, Field Marshall Sir Bernard Montgomery attributed to a bad break in the weather, which is a convenient way of passing the buck to God. The student of history might better regard the irreducible fact that the whole plan was as tight as a straitjacket, leaving almost no margin for error in the calculations of either time or space.

The costs were exacted right at the beginning, in the very hour when the airborne forces were making their first moves to capture and defend the broad highway from Eindhoven to Arnhem. The Guards Armored, which had figured on a prompt break-out from the Escaut Canal Bridgehead and a smooth advance to Eindhoven, couldn't get out of its tracks. A few German rocket men had taken a surprise position the night before in a conveniently placed copse flanking the line of advance. Their first fire brewed up a dozen tanks. The road being blocked, the attack was temporarily given over to the infantry. So it was next day—after the lapse of a fatal twenty hours—before the link-up with the airborne, which had been scheduled for that evening, was finally made at Eindhoven.

While this meager but decisive fight was going on between German rockets and British armor, 502nd Regiment was moving its main body from the assembly fields over to the main road near Zon. For the time being it was simply filling in the Division center accordion-fashion, reaching northward to link with the 501st Regiment which was to join hands with 82nd Airborne Division beyond Veghel, and reaching southward to support the 506th Regiment in its attack against the important commercial and communications center of Eindhoven.

This mission entailed covering the passage of the Wilhelmina Canal and fighting back any enemy attempt to pinch the corridor at that point. But the 506th Regiment was already sweeping the enemy from Zon while on its march to Eindhoven, and the appearance was that 502nd would have a romp until the Guards Armored rolled through.

There was one minor prick-point. The village of Best, lying 7000 yards to the west of Zon, was possessed of a bridge which would be highly useful for the passage of XXX Corps in the event the Germans blew the Zon bridge before we could seize it—as actually happened. Best was thought to contain a few squads of Germans and would therefore require a mop-up. In point of fact, about one thousand fresh troops had detrained there the day before and the line of the road running into Best at right angles to the canal was covered by six emplaced 88's, spaced at 50-yard intervals.

What developed at Best, therefore, was all consequential to what is described with classic underemphasis by the Division G2, Lieutenant Colonel Paul Danahy, as a "minor error in estimate."

It had been planned to capture Best and its bridges (the rails also crossed at this point) with one platoon. At the last moment, on request of the Battalion commander, the force was increased to one infantry company, reenforced by forty engineers. Company H started on its way while the rest of the Third Battalion was setting up in the Zon woods, and the regiment as a whole was moving into position along the main highway. Just forty-five minutes later Company H reported by radio that it was being held by enemy roadblocks. Twenty minutes passed—the time was mid-afternoon—and there came another message that it was meeting "strong resistance." The Battalion and Regiment waited, still believing that these reports were a little exaggerated.

We should now move the spotlight to the attacking column. Captain Robert E. Jones had stopped his detachment halfway between the Canal and Best to orient himself. From the Drop Zone, he had marched on Best trying to guide on the church steeple, for it was in his mind that if he could move on that line, he would hit the Canal middle distance between his main objectives, the two bridges. But the Zonsche Forest had intervened. In advancing through this pine plantation, the men had lost sight of the steeple and wandered so far off the line that they came out of the forest 600 yards north of the point which they had been seeking. Before they could veer in the intended direction, they were engaged by small arms fire from the road intersection northwest of Best. Though it grew heavier by the minute, Jones moved his men toward the fire, continuing in an approach march formation until within 200 yards of the enemy positions.

At that point the country became almost barren of cover and the men had to get down in the ditches. Realizing that he was temporarily in check and that his further advance could come only of fire and the employment of forward cover, Jones then sent his first message to Battalion.

Likewise, he decided that he would fight with one flank and proceed toward his objectives with the other, and by this step he proceeded to scatter his small forces in the face of a rapidly developing and unexpected situation.

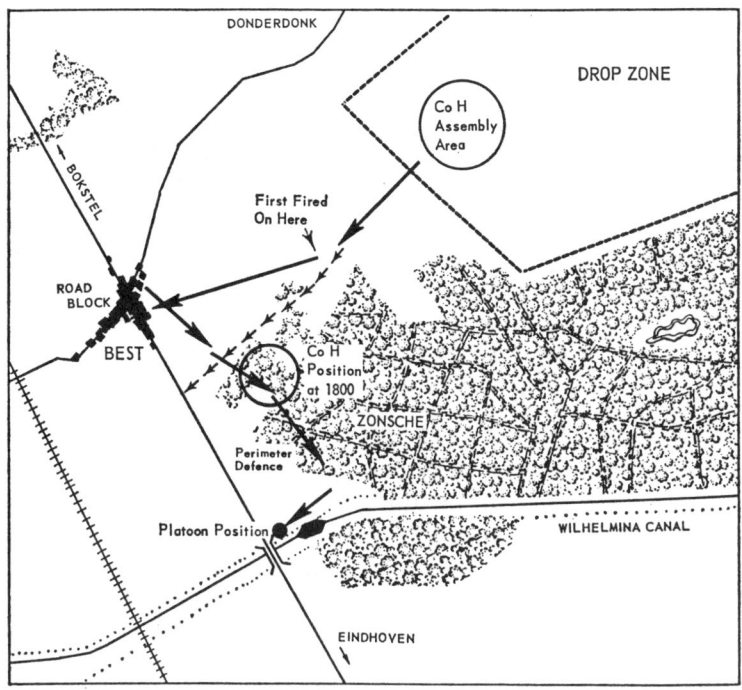

Movements on D-Day 17 September

The Second Platoon, under Lieutenant Edward L. Wierzbowski, reinforced by the detail from Company C, 326th Engineer Battalion, under Lieutenant Charles Moore, and a light machine-gun section from Battalion, was ordered to proceed to the Canal, capture the two bridges and set up defenses around them.

The First Platoon, under Lieutenant George W. Harper,

was ordered to advance on Best from the east, take the village and set up roadblocks on the north-south highway.

Company Headquarters and Third Platoon would stay in place, maintain a base of fire confronting the enemy force at the roadblock, and thereby seek to keep pressure off the two columns which were moving to its rear and flankward.

Second Platoon got duly started on its forlorn mission. But before First Platoon could do more than take a few steps toward Best, it was halted by a wave of fire from the direct front, and a number of men were hit. Nor was that the worst of it. Looking toward his right flank, Jones saw about 100 of the enemy working along the ditches and tree lines flanking the road. That left him no choice but to halt First Platoon's movement and extend his line to the northward by throwing Third Platoon into the action on its right. The line thus ran at an angle to the main road, with First Platoon directly engaging the roadblock and Third Platoon fighting the maneuver force coming along the road from the north.

At this stage Jones reported to Battalion that he was "heavily engaged"—scarcely an overstatement. But his estimate was punctuated to his full satisfaction within ten minutes. Coming toward him along the highway from the northwest, and straight into the lines of the already deployed enemy was a German truck convoy—twelve trucks and several small cannon. Jones yelled to his men to hold all fire, seeing in an instant that the enemy field force might fail to warn the motorcade, and he might get them within killing range.

A German motorcyclist was riding 250 yards in front of the trucks. He came on through the block and headed for the Canal, apparently unaware that he was running the gauntlet in a fire fight. Then came the slip-up: the Headquarters detachment had not gotten the order to suspend fire, and it shot the driver from his seat as he raced by. The convoy stopped instantly, and the Germans jumped from their trucks and deployed through the fields about 250 yards north of the block, forming a skirmish line which came on toward the Third Platoon's line under cover of a fruit orchard. On the far right of the line, Private William T. Hammond saw this movement, and he yelled to the other men: "There are two hundred more Germans coming this way." The Germans had dragged two 20-mm guns into the orchard. Their fire was now tearing the earth where the Company had settled. This simply added to the heat. The range had already been found by two pieces of artillery— one a 20-mm gun and the other an 88—which were firing from amid the gas pumps of a filling station on the edge of Best. Beset by enemy skirmishers on front and flank, the Company was now having to fight off snipers who were sifting around its rear. Staff Sergeant John J. White was dead from this fire and Lieutenants William Craig and John T. Hart were wounded and down.

Such was the twilight both of the company fight and of the day. At Battalion a decision had been made. A messenger arrived from Regiment saying that the Battalion was authorized to support Company H. The Battalion commander, Lieutenant Colonel Robert H. Cole, had gone to higher authority asking that sanction. According to the regimental commander, Colonel John T. Michaelis, the request was denied, and Cole acted strictly on his own. It does not matter now. The Battalion proceeded, temporarily under the command of its executive, Major John P. Stopka. As the Company had marched directly from the Drop Zone, and the Battalion moved from well to the south of that area where it had been holding the woods near Zon, it did not traverse the same route, but followed approximately the line of the Canal.

Dark was just closing down as Cole caught up with his men. They were marching alongside the dike about one mile east of Best. As he took over from Stopka, the head of the column was suddenly checked by rifle and machine-gun fire. The men went flat and began to dig in. At Cole's order, Company

G sent a half squad under Sergeant Delwin McKimmy to try to contact Company H and reconnoiter the source of the fire. That done, he moved the battalion into the Zonsche Forest where Captain Jones had gone astray, and the men dug in solid for the night with their main line near the western edge of the woods and facing toward Best. So situated, they were within 1000 yards or less of where Company H was having its nose bloodied. Captain Jones, though getting approximately nowhere, was at least becoming more hopeful. Battalion continued to get radio reports that he was "nearing the objective" when in fact he was only holding on and wishing for help. But Battalion couldn't figure out his location that night, and the broad day had to come before McKimmy's patrol was able to find its way to Jones's lines. Faced with an unequal struggle, Jones had decided a little too late to pull in his horns.

There had been a spattering of small arms fire throughout the night. At first light the volume increased heavily, the firing coming mainly from the highway east of Best, and the Battalion began to take casualties. When McKimmy returned with the news of Company H, Cole advanced the Battalion and its lines were soon tied-in to the position which Jones had maintained, 1000 yards south of his earlier position.

But there was one thing that McKimmy could not tell Cole—the fate of the Second Platoon which had been sent off under Wierzbowski to capture the Best bridges. It had simply vanished into the darkness and no word had come back.

It is now necessary therefore to follow the strange and savage fortunes of this small band of men who were handed a mission far beyond their compass, and whose attempt to cope with it is as replete with heroism and irony as any tale to be told of our forces in World War II.

Wierzbowski was a little confused right from the beginning. An intensely earnest soldier, he shared Jones's fault of seeing too many things at one time. Having been told to get the bridges, he became distracted, as he moved out, by the same sniper fire which was giving hell to the Company rear. He decided to take one squad and try to advance along the hedgerow toward Best, figuring that his movement would compel the snipers to give ground. However, as this advance would clear the ground over only a small radius, he told Lieutenant Andrew P. Duffy to take one rifle squad, one squad of engineers and the section of machine guns about 200 yards to his left and then proceed toward Best along a line paralleling his own. He had but barely started along the hedgerow when he called Jones by radio and told him what he was doing. Jones promptly and rightly recalled him. He then sought to rejoin Duffy, who by this change of orders had been put well out on a limb.

Whatever Duffy's strengths, he was a weak judge of distance. Instead of 200, he had moved 500 yards to the southeast before turning back to the road. This line took him through a heavy pine growth. The men were just well into the trees when they heard 20-mm fire cracking the branches above them. So they stopped to consider. Thus gone motionless, they could hear Germans talking to one another some forty or fifty yards beyond. Duffy told the machine-gun section to advance and set up along the far edge of woods. From that cover, he looked into a farmyard and saw a group of Germans gathered around the 20-mm piece. The four machine guns all opened fire at one time.

The range was less than 150 yards. But only two Germans fell. Within a split second—so fast that it was clear that the enemy had kept almost exact touch with Duffy's advance—three 20-mm guns mounted on halftracks whipped around from behind the farmhouse and barn and opened fire.

Four men at the machine guns were felled by the first burst. Corporal Willis Hart yelled to Duffy: "We're all going to be killed." Duffy shouted: "Work back toward the Company!"

Lieutenant Robert Lair picked up a machine gun and tried to get across the road with it to cover the withdrawal. As he did so, another 20-mm gun opened fire from the right flank, and the men saw Lair go down. Corporal William T. Nichols went down, hit five times by bullets. Private Wesley E. Jackson crawled out of the woods carrying Nichols on his back, and while he was crawling, a sixth bullet hit Nichols. Such infantrymen as were not wounded had already cleared the wood. But the engineers, who had come in on the left with one machine gun, didn't see the withdrawal, and save for two men, they stayed there with the gun through the night.

This brief skirmish reveals the reality of the pressure that Jones was feeling on his left and rear. We have already seen that what was happening to his right and center was far from a Sunday school picnic. Further than that, lest unfair criticism be heaped upon him, it should be added that Battalion, without knowing much about the situation, had arbitrarily insisted that the Wierzbowski force should be detached and sent to the bridges.

But it took this flare-up of action around Duffy's men to make Jones see that the order had put him "between the devil and the deep blue sea," as he himself expressed it. Clearly he was asking for complete ruin if he tried to fight on ground where he was opposed from three sides while sending Wierzbowski off on a wild goose chase. Wierzbowski told him on radio that he was standing on ground right then that was highly suitable for defense. Jones took him at his word, and got the company in motion toward the Canal, with the remaining engineers and Headquarters detachment leading off, followed by the Third and First Platoons. The Germans did not press them during the withdrawal. The body of the Company took over from Second Platoon in a small neck of woods, then set up a perimeter defense about fifty yards in circumference. After that Wierzbowski went on his way, hoping to wrest two bridges from the German Army in the darkness with his shrunken command. It was already a badly depleted body, made so not only by fire losses but by Duffy's having taken the wrong line again. In his fall-back from the little woods where he had been routed, toward the main woods which the Company had crossed earlier in the afternoon, Duffy had again come under fire. His men had fled for this cover and were now scattered. Wierzbowski sent runners into the forest but the search was unavailing.

Just as the sun went down, Wierzbowski led his column into this planting of young pine, where fire-breaks spaced at 35-yard intervals provided the only interruption to the evenly checkered rows. They met fire before the column had walked its own length into the forest. The enemy had filtered into the plantation during the afternoon and had spaced machine guns so that together they now covered some of the fire-breaks for their entire length; the forest floor was perfectly flat; there was no way of knowing at which of the lanes the Platoon would draw fire.

Thus in a sweat to get to the bridges before the last light faded, Wierzbowski was at the same time in a situation where he had to exercise restraint on his men lest they become scattered and immobilized by sudden fire. He told them to move slowly and check at each lane; then they were to bound forward one man at a time until the whole platoon was clear. This made the whole march slow and plodding, with a fresh start called for every thirty-five yards. But it seemed to be worth it. The Germans had set up machine guns so as to cover every third or fourth fire-break, and the guns started popping whenever the lead man started across. Yet the Platoon—eighteen men from Company H and twenty-six engineers—made this unhappy passage without a casualty. They came at last to the final lane and they sprinted across it in a body, with two guns barking at them vainly.

Now it was necessary to advance in the open, and they

did this on hands and knees. While moving at the crawl, they were joined by a few of Lair's men—including three walking wounded. They had been hiding in the bush and when they heard Wierzbowski's scouts call out to him, they came as fast as they could.

The advance was now over ground which was slightly rolling. Shortly thereafter, the hard earth gave way to marsh. Feeling his way in the pitch black of a rainy night, the first scout, Private Joe E. Mann, skirted far over to the left and came out on the dike bounding the Wilhelmina Canal. He sent word back by the second scout, Private James C. Hoyle, that there was a hard surface road atop the dike. Wierzbowski led his men up and onto the road at a point about 500 yards east of the highway bridge.

The Bridge at Best

In the foreground loomed several large derricks and other objects which could not be distinguished except for their mass. The men crawled slowly along, trying to feel their way through this canal-side loading zone. There was a catwalk suspended out over the Canal and around the derricks. The column chanced it, and for those minutes in which they made this desperate circuit, they hardly breathed; had a flare gone up, they would have been just so many sitting ducks. The hour was then about 2100. The walk was clay-covered and slippery. Such were the unique difficulties of this journey that they used more than one hour in closing the last 500 yards.

The thing seemed to be within reach—perhaps another thirty yards or so—when a few rounds of rifle fire blazed out of the darkness, from directly in front. Still, it was not followed up, and the fire had gone well over the heads of the party. Wierzbowski concluded that he had not been discovered. So he crawled up to the lead scout to see if the bridge was there and to determine if anyone was guarding it. Putting his lips next to Mann's ear, he whispered: "I think we're all right; come along."

The two men crawled forward together for only a few paces, but it was just a few paces too far!

At that exact moment, the Germans covering the bridge had been changing guard. The old sentry had withdrawn to the bridge entrance. Thus the two men missed him. But the new man came on back and passed them. They saw him swing in a wide circle around them and they realized that they were squatting right in the middle of his sentry post.

It was like a hard kick in the groin. They could not jump him; there was a second guard on the far side of the stream who kept shouting back and forth to this man, and firing his rifle after every few turns. Nor could they get out; they were so close to the sentry that the least movement was certain to reveal them.

So for many minutes (all hands agree that this wait must have exceeded a half-hour) they stayed there, motionless and not knowing what to do. Not one word passed between them in all that time. They were shaken as hell and they simply waited for a break to come. The sentry, continuing to make the circle around them, did not act as if he had the slightest suspicion that an enemy force was right at hand.

But back along the side of the dike where the men of the platoon were waiting, this unnerving situation was reacting on the others in quite the opposite fashion. Not knowing what had happened to the two-man advance party, they thought they should do something about it. The second in command, Lieutenant Watson, thought he ought to give an order, but didn't know what order to give. The men were stirring, and their whispering grew louder. While they waited, several potato masher grenades were tossed from the far side of the Canal and exploded on the dike above them. But they took this as coincidence rather than as a warning.

The issue was decided when two men got up and started to scramble up the embankment. The others began to rise. Watson gave some kind of order half-heartedly, but the men didn't get it, and they kept on going.

Private Joseph Perkins was the fourth man to reach the top of the dike. As he straightened up, the enemy opened fire on the Americans with machine guns and rifles from the opposite bank. Perkins fell back, hit in the shoulder.

He was the only casualty. Even so, what had happened was enough to stampede a majority of the party. They ran like mad in the general direction whence they had come, and what further fate befell the runaways that night is still not known.

The die-hards ran down the side of the dike and began to dig in right at the base. That operation was stopped by Wierzbowski, who made them fall back about sixty yards from the dike before setting up their defensive position. He and Mann had been given a sudden release from their strange confinement when the fire broke out; they jumped up and ran toward the fire while the sentry was still gaping in that direction. On the run, Wierzbowski counted five machine guns firing toward his men.

Artillery and mortar shells were exploding around them while they dug. Wierzbowski looked his force over: of the fifteen men and three officers remaining, three were already wounded. Of heavier weapons, he had one machine gun with 500 rounds, one mortar with six rounds and one bazooka with five rounds.

The rain continued. At 0300 the enemy fire ceased for the night. Even then, Wierzbowski made no effort to lead his men out and rejoin the company. He had roughly counted the odds against himself, but he had been given an order, and it was in his mind that he must try again for the bridge if daylight showed it still standing.

Back at the company, Jones had been getting an insistent prodding by radio from Battalion. "God damn it, send someone to find Wierzbowski!" So he had ordered out two patrols, and finally had sent the Third Platoon, much against Jones's better judgment. These prowls were absolutely futile, and each of them was beaten back by fire. Nor was there any more relief within the company perimeter. Mortar and artillery continued to find them through the night, and by the hour of first light another thirty men had been killed or wounded.

From what he saw of the enemy strength and fire during the night, Cole at last concluded that he could forget about the lost platoon. He said to Stopka: "They've been annihilated beyond a doubt."

The Lost Patrol

Early on the second morning of the fight at Best, Colonel John T. Michaelis, commanding 502nd Regiment, came from Zon to the Zonsche Forest where Lieutenant Colonel "Bob" Cole had bivouacked Third Battalion, looked the scene over, and decided that he had better commit his Second Battalion on Cole's right flank in an effort to clean up the fight and free Cole's forces.

The fortunes of all forces in Operation Market Garden were thus staked altogether around the Wilhelmina Canal on the outcome of a struggle which in the beginning had seemed to call for nothing more than a foray by a platoon. Michaelis had no further reserve, his First Battalion being already engaged to the hilt in a fight for St.-Oedenrode, farther to the north. Moreover, the British XXX Corps column had not yet come through and our own forces had not yet captured Eindhoven. This meant that the grand design was already wasting away by the hour and that further hurt to it was being threatened in every tactically decisive area.

By 0800 when Lieutenant Colonel Steve A. Chappuis got his Second Battalion on march from Zon, Cole's lines were taking such a beating from mortar and artillery fire that he had to order his men to fall back deeper into the woods. It was Michaelis' idea that Chappuis should march his column north and then sweep toward Best from out of the northeast, so that as his attack started, his line would be in echelon to the right of Cole's position.

This was what he attempted, with his object being to drive on into Best and then swing south to the bridges. His own companies were echeloned to the right rear as the attack started. They drew artillery fire immediately but kept going toward the Bokstel-Eindhoven highway.

What happened during the next few minutes has been repeatedly praised as the one shining example from World War II in which American tactical forces acted exactly according to the book.

The Dutch had been haying and the fields confronting Chappuis were covered by small piles of hay, three to four feet in height. These piles were the only cover, for the fields were absolutely flat. From left to right the line rippled forward in perfect order and well-timed discipline, each group of two or three men running on to the next hay pile as it came their turn. Machine-gun fire cut into the hay piles, sometimes setting the cover afire, sometimes wounding or killing the men who lay behind it. That stopped only the dead and the wounded. The squad leaders kept leading and the platoon leaders kept shouting to each group when to make a dash for it. It was like a problem worked out on a parade ground, and of course the even setting of the hay piles was one of the factors that made it so.

But Chappuis had finally to give over, not because his men were unwilling, but because he realized that his mortal losses were beating him. It was clear that while he might get as far as the highway, the price would be the destruction of his Battalion. The moral of that morning's fight is that safety lies forward only when the tactical odds are reasonably even. The whole area of the attack was being rent by artillery, mortar and automatic fire. To this the Battalion was able to reply only with its own mortars. Eight of the officers already lay strewn in the hay field and 21 per cent of the men were already dead or wounded when Chappuis decided to stop the advance, call his men back and reorganize.

Michaelis concluded later that he erred in sending Chap-

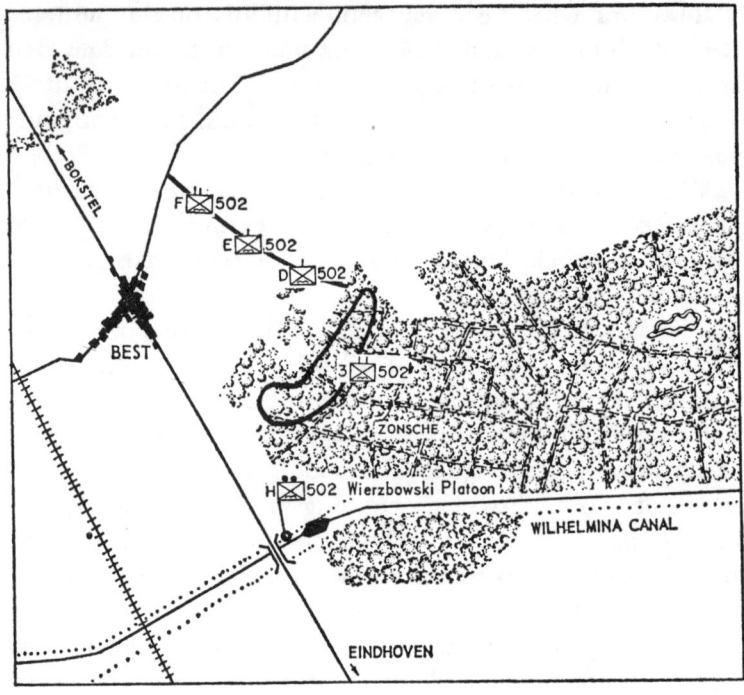

Situation at 10 A.M. 18 September

puis forward on this line instead of having him close directly on Third Battalion and attack under a covering fire from Cole's men. But until Second Battalion met the reality head-on, the strength of the enemy around Best had been estimated at only one-third of its true weight.

Nor was it lacking in aggressive quality. Cole was again having a bad experience. His withdrawal to the deep wood had been accepted by the Germans as an invitation to filter back through the western tree line. Their snipers kept him between a chill and a sweat. He could not tighten his lines to the point where all companies were well contained on account of the constant artillery fire. He could not loosen them more than was already done because the enemy was coming by twos and threes into his lines, as now organized.

A strong and persistent force worked into the ground between Companies G and H, and both companies began to lose men from close-up rifle fire.

Cole called to Regiment to see if he could get air support against the Germans who were coming across the highway and into the woods. Then he left his foxhole to apprise Stopka of what he had done. In his absence, a shell landed next to the hole, and a part of it exploded through the skull of Cole's radio operator. Cole was wiping the blood and brains from the radio when Stopka came by a few minutes later to tell him that some P-47's were coming over. Fortunately the radio was still working.

By this time enemy snipers were firing directly on the CP and the Battalion had become almost inert. Cole shouted to his men but most of them would not leave the foxholes to take countermeasures. Mortar and artillery fire, though as great a danger to the Germans in the woods as to Cole's men, seemed to harass only the one side. What seemed at first only random sniper fire had now the proportions of a counterattack.

The P-47's came low to strafe. Their bullet fire began to rake the Battalion position in the woods. Stopka went running to get the men busy with panels; they had to improvise the panels on the spot out of orange flags. A call came over the radio for Stopka; Cole sent for him and then went out to take over the work which Stopka had been doing.

He got the job almost completed. The P-47's began to find the enemy lines with their strafing attack, and there was a sudden and notable let-down in the volume of enemy fire from beyond the highway. Cole walked out in front of his men and beyond the woods. For a brief period, he stood there deliberately in the open, with his hand shielding his eyes, looking up at a circling plane.

Then a sniper's bullet from a house 100 yards away hit him through the temple and he died instantly. It was the not-unexpected ending for a young leader, Texas born and

West Point educated, who had won the Congressional Medal in the fight at Carentan and had continued to set for his battalion an example of personal bravery which was frequently at odds with any well-rounded concept of his administrative responsibilities.

Lieutenant Ralph A. Watson was a few paces in rear of Cole when he was shot. Such was the emotional hold which Cole had on many of his men that young Watson couldn't make himself phrase the words: "Cole is dead." So to Stopka he sent only this word by messenger: "You are in command of the Battalion." Stopka worked on for another hour, thinking it was only a temporary matter.

A German ran from the corner of the house where the sniper had fired on Cole. A Battalion machine gun cut him down in mid-flight. Though nobody could be sure about the matter, the word was passed from foxhole to foxhole that the Battalion had finished the man who had killed Cole. That made everyone feel better.

Between Chappuis' sweep and the fight which attended the strafing attack by the P-47's, however, one important tactical effect had been achieved which was to benefit the last stages of the battle. Small parties of Americans were in hiding at several points in the woods—the strays who had been lost the night before by Duffy's action and the part of Captain Jones's line that had failed to make the initial withdrawal with the rest of the Company. From their hideouts they observed that these pressures along the northern side of the forest were gradually flushing the enemy down toward its southern extremity and that a considerable concentration of manpower was building there.

The immediate tactical effect, however, was to complete the isolation of Wierzbowski and his eighteen men in their beleaguered outpost alongside the Wilhelmina dike, since this large working force of the enemy was now interposed directly between them and the main body of the Regiment.

As the morning wore along, they saw these skirmishers

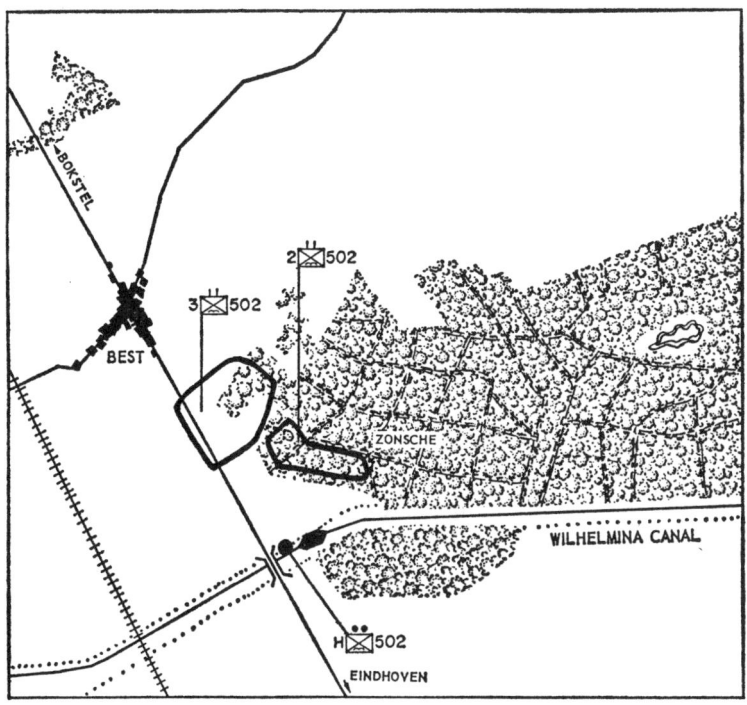

Situation at 8 P.M. 18 September

working toward them from out of the forest. Wierzbowski passed the word around for his men to hold their fire. When the Germans got to within less than fifty yards, the order was given to open up with all weapons. They saw about thirty-five men fall at the volley, the machine gun having cut a wide swath, after which the remainder of the line faded back to the woods. So they scored even though the Platoon was being pressed from two sides at one time. There was a German barracks just twenty yards from the bridge and south of the Canal, with manned rifle pits around it. Another group of the enemy was entrenched eighty yards away on the far side of the highway. If a man arose from his foxhole to stretch, or to start toward the Canal, he at once drew fire from two sides.

As for the bridge, it was still intact, a beautifully styled one-span concrete structure, perhaps 150 feet in length. This was the whole object of their striving. It was only sixty yards away—not more than a 20-second sprint from their foxholes. They had no choice but to lie there and look at it.

About mid-morning, the watching men saw a German soldier and a civilian come up to the far side of the bridge and stand there for perhaps twenty minutes, talking animatedly. They thought little of the incident; in any event, they could not get a clear shot at the soldier. Exactly at 1100 hours, there was a deafening explosion. The concrete span shook, lifted and fell into the water. The men had to bend low in their foxholes as concrete and steel debris from the blast fell all around them. The pair whom they had watched earlier at the bridge had been maneuvering to set a time fuse to an already prepared demolition. But there was no way to get word of this denouement to the Regiment. The latter continued to act on the assumption that the bridge was a prize still within reach, and that Wierzbowski had been destroyed.

The two scouts, Mann and Hoyle, who had been leading the fight from the beginning, made one spectacular sortie. About one hundred yards west of the foxholes was a German artillery dump. They crawled toward it and set it off with two rounds from the bazooka. Hoyle saw immediately that this ground was so formed that it was secure against anything save grenades tossed from the other side of the Canal. So they holed up there and in one hour shot six Germans coming toward them from the north. Then Mann was hit twice by rifle bullets—once through each shoulder—and he reacted by passing the bazooka to Hoyle, telling him to try his luck. About 150 yards up the Canal an 88-mm was firing eastward. Hoyle had the good luck to hit and destroy it with the first round.

The P-47's which Cole had requested flew over the position about noontime. The platoon could hear the regimental fight in the distance, but seeing nothing of it, they imagined that the battalions were on the march to them and that they would be relieved before sundown.

In mid-afternoon, the Germans pressed an attack toward them along the Canal bank. The position was drawing heavy fire; the men were trying to return it, but couldn't get a good line on its source. Lieutenant Watson of the Engineers scouted out front to get a better view of the attack. He was hit in the abdomen and went down. First-aid man Private Orvac crawled out and treated him, then called to Wierzbowski. Watson thought his testicles had been shot off and he begged Wierzbowski to shoot him with his .45 pistol. Wierzbowski dragged him 150 yards back to the lines, looked him over carefully and told him to be happy, that his testicles were all right.

Private Luther was hit and killed by a shell fragment in the head. Private Mann was hit by two more bullets. Both of his arms had to be put in slings. But he begged Wierzbowski to leave him with the active defenders instead of putting him in the large foxhole with the immobilized wounded; he got his wish. Private Northrup, hit in the base of the spine, died from loss of blood. By now the detachment was wholly out of bandages and medicine. Sergeant Betras of the Engineers volunteered to try to break through for aid. A few minutes later, Betras returned, wounded in the head. He had been ambushed.

As for the "big picture" in these hours, matters were slightly on the mend. The British XXX Corps armor had come at last into Eindhoven, the American 506th Regiment having already captured that city. As the situation in the south became more snug, there was renewed hope that the forces beyond the Rhine near Arnhem would be able to hold out for the required interval, and that all would work out well in the end.

It made a difference—even to Wierzbowski.

A British armored car, accompanied by a reconnaisance

car, had whipped out some miles in advance of the XXX Corps column; this of itself was no great feat, as 506th Regiment had cleared the road from Zon to Eindhoven.

Getting to Zon and finding the bridge blown, the British cars came down the dike, looking for the Best bridge. Quite suddenly they were there, on the far side of the Canal. Wierzbowski yelled across and told them of his situation. He asked them to raise Division on radio and explain his plight, but they couldn't manage to get through.

The Germans, reacting slowly to the appearance of the two cars, at last opened fire. Both cars then pulled back behind the corner of the barracks and blazed away with their machine guns. The effect was surprising: the German force on the far bank quit their foxholes and withdrew westward.

Corporal Daniel L. Corman found a small boat on the bank, rowed over to the armored car, and came back with a medical kit.

That gave Wierzbowski an idea. He told his men to get up, and they would all row across the Canal and retreat eastward under the protection of the armored car.

But the car commander shouted across to him: "Stay where you are! I am sure that help will be here very soon." He said that he would stay there and cover them until a relief arrived, and on that promise, the Wierzbowski group settled back into their foxholes.

Before the night settled, Regiment was to make one more try toward capturing the bridge which was no longer there. In late afternoon, Chappuis, having completed his reorganization, was ordered to attack southeast on the east side of the Best-Eindhoven highway, pass through Third Battalion and continue toward the bridge. Third Battalion was ordered to support this attack with fire until the fire was masked.

The attack went off unevenly. But one platoon from Company D under Lieutenant Mottola had such clear sailing that it kept right on barreling down the road. Shortly after

2300 hours, Mottola and his men tied into Wierzbowski's position at the dike, and settled down on his left flank. For Wierzbowski, this was the third bright event of the evening. An hour earlier, a patrol from Company E had reached his lines and had told him of having heard from Company H that his platoon had been wiped out. He told them to get back to Battalion with the word that he was still in operation, but had so many wounded on his hands that they would have to come to him. And here occurs one of the most painful lapses in the operation: by the time this patrol's report got up to Chappuis (which did not occur until next morning, the patrol having got lost in the woods), it conveyed only the intelligence that the Best bridge had been blown, and said nothing about the lost platoon.

With Mottola's arrival, Wierzbowski's group concluded that their worst hours were over. Completely exhausted, they dozed in their foxholes, and left it to Mottola's men to cover them, since the newcomers were facing to the westward.

In the middle of the night, this force which was holding the outwork was suddenly beset by a German attack pressed from the direction of Best. Mottola's line broke and the men fell back across the Canal, some of them swimming and others crawling across the wrecked bridge. They ultimately recrossed the Canal far to the eastward and it was two days before the survivors got back to the Battalion.

Only their state of absolute exhaustion can explain the fact that Wierzbowski's men slept through this attack hardly aware that anything untoward had happened. Wierzbowski awakened hearing men splashing through the Canal and shouting to one another as they reached the far bank. This was the first he knew that his left flank had departed.

To complete their misfortunes, the British armored car, hearing Americans come into the position during the night, had concluded that the relief was accomplished and had pulled away from the far bank.

So once again, they sat in their foxholes, alerted themselves as best they could and waited for morning. They knew that the Second Battalion attack, from which Mottola's group had been cut loose and cast forward, had brought a goodly portion of the Regiment's strength to within squeezing distance of the bridge.

There was thus good reason to believe that all of the night's confusions would be lifted when morning came. Not being psychic, they couldn't foresee that though every kind of bad luck had cursed them from the beginning, the worst still awaited them.

About Joe Mann

On the third morning of the fight at Best, as the light began to break, the general situation of the American forces seemed for the first time to be on the upgrade.

During the preceding stages of the struggle, they had been fighting blind in the Zonsche Forest, with enemy forces either directly engaging them or harassing them with small arms and artillery fire from three sides.

These forbidding conditions were now gradually being absolutely reversed. The attack of Second Battalion on the prior evening toward the bridge along the southwest corner of the forest had almost wholly relieved the distress of Third Battalion. Simultaneously, the latter had struck on its own account and patrols from Company I had crossed the highway to the westward, dug in on the far side, and put a block on the road.

In consequence, what remained of the enemy forces along the highway to the south of this point thereupon withdrew. To the north, however, the enemy was still lost in the fog of war and becoming a victim of his own communications. The word did not reach him that the Americans had cut the road. On the stroke of midnight, an armored car with forty men behind it moved straight into the Company I roadblock. The armored car actually had its bumper pressing against the logs when the Company I men along the ditches on both sides opened fire. Ten Germans were slain and most of the others were captured. The armored car backed away quick as a flash and escaped.

That night the American lines at Bivouac had about the same ingenious pattern as a pretzel. Second Battalion was fronted southeastward, set for defense, but ready to resume at 0600 hours its attack toward the bridge. Company G of Third Battalion was backstopping this position. Company I was stretched from the forest to across the highway, confronting Best, and defending to the northwestward. Company H was in extension of the Company I line, but on a reversed curve which enabled its open flank to give partial protection to the troops which faced south and eastward. The mortars were in the center of the general position.

The one spot of unrelieved black in this otherwise brightening situation was the plight of Wierzbowski's lost detachment at the bridge, of which Regiment still knew nothing. Materially, they had reached the end of the string, though morally, they were still in the fight. They had come to the last of their ammunition; most of their number were now either dead or made helpless by wounds. The one remaining chance was that Chappuis, attacking with Second Battalion, would reach them in time.

This chance died almost at its moment of birth. The attack started on time. Immediately thereafter, the patrol from Company E which had learned about Wierzbowski the night before and then lost itself in the woods, re-entered the Regimental lines, bringing the word that the bridge was down. This seemed to deny the attack any purpose, and it was stopped. Though we may remark with wonder upon the failure of this patrol to report the plight of the lost platoon, the incident is not exceptional. Troops are ever disposed to take a compassionate interest in the hardships of members of "their own" company or battalion while remaining quite indifferent to the fate of men from other units.

In their position next the dike, Wierzbowski and his men first looked at the morning through a mist so thick that they could see the ruined bridge only in outline. They were alone, but they were so tired that they made no move to redistribute themselves so as to cover the gap in their defenses caused by Mottola's abrupt departure.

The light grew, and at last the sun broke through the mist, seeming to roll it up like a curtain.

Wierzbowski looked around him. Just twenty feet away, he saw a German officer. A line of men was following him. Wierzbowski yelled. Sergeant Betras threw a grenade. Several of the others threw also.

But the enemy had beaten them to these same tactics and several grenades were already rolling down into the foxholes. Two of them hit the embankment of the large foxhole and rolled down among the wounded. Betras threw the first one out. Someone else threw out the other. A third grenade went wild.

The fourth grenade hit the machine gun and exploded directly into the face of the gunner, Private Laino, blinding him.

Private Lawrence Koller and Corman were together in a foxhole. A bullet hit Koller in the temple. He gasped heavily for a moment, then slumped and lay still, and Corman thought he was dead. He yelled for the aid man. Laino, too, was crying: "Aid man! Aid man!" But the one medic had sprung to help Koller, and there was no one, and no time, to help the wounded machine gunner.

Then the men saw another grenade loop over Wierzbowski's head, hit Laino on the knee, and roll off into his foxhole. They saw Laino, blinded as he was, reach down groping for it, and while they had their split-second agony of suspense, his hand found it and tossed it out, just before it exploded in mid-air.

The next grenade fell behind Private Mann. He sat at the back of the trench, a large trench holding six other men. His voice called "Grenade!" as the missile looped over and settled in the dirt. But both of his arms were bound from his four wounds of the day before and he could not reach for it. So he deliberately lay back on the grenade, yelling to the others: "I'm taking this one!" It exploded into his back, blew fragments into the side and belly of Private Anthony Atayde and wounded Privates Paxton and Wienz each in the hip. Mann said quietly to Wierzbowski: "My back's gone," and a minute or two later he died, without a groan or whimper.

For saving the lives of his comrades, Private Mann was posthumously awarded the Congressional Medal by a grateful government. The perfect tribute was given by the survivors who said that his peerless courage during the three days had proved their chief rallying point.

One last grenade was thrown. It exploded a cloud of dust and sand in front of the position. The enemy came running forward. The men had kept asking Wierzbowski: "Do we quit or fight?" They asked no question this time, but he gave his answer. Their own last grenade was gone. Only three of the men remained unwounded. Either they surrendered now or all would be killed.

Wierzbowski said: "OK. This is the time." Private Anthony M. Waldt put a dirty handkerchief on his carbine and waved it. The fire ceased.

The men, including the wounded, were told to come crawling from their foxholes, and to continue in that posture as they moved westward along the side of the dike. The Germans had heard the noise of Second Battalion's attack in the not-distant foreground, and were fearful of attracting attention. But Laino was bleeding too badly to make the start. Wierzbowski told a German NCO about Laino, and he dropped his rifle, bandaged him, and helped carry him out.

Corman and Koller were overlooked in this movement. Thinking Koller dead, when the surrender came, Corman dropped across him and played dead. Thus they lay there from early morning until 1630 hours, not moving. American artillery pounded this ground hard throughout the afternoon. A German machine-gun crew arrived at mid-day, casually regarded the two men, set up their gun next the hole, and fired for several hours. When the general American advance overran this ground late in the day, Corman was still whole and Koller was salvaged. At least, there was still a spark of life in him.

The rest of the party, save one, were taken to an earth mound west of the highway, behind which the Germans kept them under guard and tried to doctor their wounds. The exception was Private Hoyle, who, lagging a little behind the party and pretending that he was hard hit, got only as far as the road. There he dropped into a foxhole and pulled a few branches over him. Another enemy machine-gun party took position within six feet of him and operated there for eight hours. He, too, was freed by the general American advance. He immediately found himself a rifle and a few clips and went back into the battle.

After having his attack called off, Chappuis had returned Second Battalion to its line of departure. There he was twice counterattacked during the morning, the Germans coming up the trail through the little wood where Duffy had had his misadventure.

In the interim, however, as Chappuis' weight had shifted more to the southwestward, Company G's position in the forest had become uncovered, and enemy forces, coming from the direction of the Drop Zone, began to press against its left flank. Lieutenant Donald Irwin led a sally with the First Platoon in an effort to clear the company front of this harassment. As he gained the edge of the woods and broke out onto the open field, Irwin was hit on the head by a 20-mm shell. For four hours he lay there, an easy target for enemy skirmishers who kept crawling to the edge of the wood to take potshots at him. Staff Sergeant Allen W. Jones, feeling that he would get the platoon slaughtered if he advanced it into the open to rescue Irwin, took on as a personal task the elimination of the enemy party. He crawled out beyond the lines and through the forest, keeping watch until at last he got a line on the source of the fire against Irwin. There were ten Germans, working together, most of them armed with machine pistols. He killed them one man at a time. Irwin had fourteen bullet holes in him when his men were at last able to go out and drag him back—at least a little bit alive.

During all these hours, however, the "big picture" was changing momentously, British XXX Corps' main column was passing on the main highway to the east of the Zonsche Forest, and artillery and armored help were now at hand. The 327th Glider Infantry Regiment, landing as the Division reenforcement, was ordered at once to advance in support of 502nd Regiment. They got into action almost as soon as the march started. While Third Battalion was moving across the flat country near Melenkampen, its scouts got into a brush with an enemy force of 200 men advancing south to join the fight in the Zonsche Forest.

Third Battalion wasn't expecting a meeting engagement and had no way of deploying in time to produce an envelopment, since both forces were moving in the same direction. But the companies attacked in parallel columns echeloned to the left rear, with all columns hitting at the enemy rear. The Germans fled in panic, leaving seventy-five prisoners and a number of dead. Those who managed to survive and escape this fight were caught in the grinder farther south in the Zonsche Forest.

For with the arrival of these fresh forces, the enemy groups which still maneuvered east of Best were now held tight in a giant man-trap. The 327th came straight on and formed a line along the north fringe of the wood. The British armor was moving north on the road from Zon, thus preventing escape to the east. The 502nd Regiment was covering the road on the west and the Wilhelmina Canal barred passage to the south.

At 1100 hours a squadron of the 15/19 Hussars, from the

British column, was placed in support of 327th Regiment by 101st Division, and 16 tanks were immediately dispatched to 502nd Regiment for use in an attack by all forces which was set for 1415 hours.

Stopka and Chappuis conferred. The decision was that each battalion would attack with six tanks. Company I would put a platoon behind three tanks at the left of the road, and Company G, similarly supported, would advance on the left of Company I. As this line came parallel to Second Battalion, it would form with six tanks and extend the sweep. At the same time, Second Battalion, 327th Regiment, would push two forces south and west through the forest from its northern extremity, continuing as far as the Canal. Turning its back to this movement, Third Battalion, 327th Regiment, would advance north to deal with any possible attempt at reenforcement.

Thus the plan. Company I's tanks happened to arrive first and the platoon jumped off before anyone could tell it no. The tanks at once shelled the wood with their 17-pounders. Fearing that his attack was going off half-cocked, Stopka went running to stop the advance of his right. Before he could bark an order, seventy-five Germans came out of the woods with their hands in air. Seeing in a flash that the whole situation was suddenly turning, Stopka saved his breath. The tanks and the platoon went right on along, and more men arose from the paths and ditches in the foreground. A few had to be killed by the fire; the majority was completely demoralized. Convinced that the "rumble of the tanks and the noise of their fire" had taken all heart from the enemy, Stopka called Regiment, saying: "Send me every MP you have."

By the time the single platoon came abreast of Company G and the Battalion attack started as a whole, there were already 100 prisoners in the bag. Second Battalion, taking the cue, had also thrown co-ordination to the winds and had lashed out with its six tanks without waiting for Stopka's

line to come abreast. It had shaken 300 prisoners out of the
woods before it was well started.

Chappuis, moving along with his Battalion, was unfor-
gettably impressed by the swift demoralization wrought by
the arrival of the armor. There were only a few bitter-
enders who insisted on making the defeat blacker than it was
by nature. Not once "but ten times," Chappuis saw men
arise from the enemy position with their hands in air, only
to be mowed down by the machine-gun fire of their comrades while they were trying to surrender.

In all parts of the Zonsche sector, the rest of the operation was hardly more than a mop-up. In two hours, Second
Battalion captured 700 prisoners. Third Battalion didn't

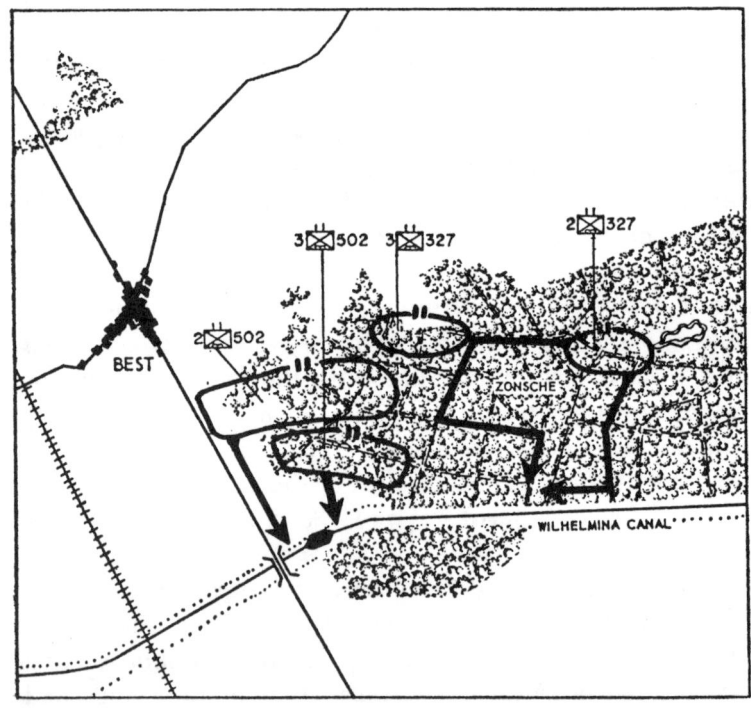

Co-ordinated Attacks 19 September

bother to keep a count, Stopka telling his men to let the prisoners sift on back and he would find some way to take care of them. A scratch detail of cooks and clerks was rounded up by the Battalion executive, Captain Frank Lillyman, to hold the bag until the MP's arrived. By that time the bag held 1100 of the enemy. Sweeping south through the Zonsche Forest, Company G, 327th Regiment, using two platoons, captured an additional 159 Germans, and killed "quite a number" without taking a casualty.

In the late afternoon, Stopka had a detail of his men take a census of the battlefield. There were 600 German bodies scattered over the ground between the southern fringes of the forest and the Canal.

The advance by the tanks and the infantry line went as far as the dike. Then Lieutenant Baker took the Company I platoon to the west of the highway and cleared out the wood patches on that side for a distance of about 400 yards. But they did not go into Best. A force of about 700 of the enemy continued to hold out there during the succeeding days while Operation Market-Garden was being written off as a strategic failure because of the defeat at Arnhem. They still held Best during the succeeding weeks while 101st Division was fighting on "The Island" north of Nijmegen. It made no difference; the Corridor was safe, and these enemy people weren't going anywhere.

There is one last note. While the battle went on toward its sputtering conclusion, Wierzbowski and his few survivors, in the position where they were kept prisoner behind the mound, saw wounded Germans flocking to the rear looking for first aid men. A few stopped at the mound to ask for help. One was the German NCO who had bandaged Laino that morning; he was now hard hit in the shoulder. They gave him such help as was possible.

From the mound the Wierzbowski group was taken to a German field hospital between the highway and Best. When the tanks began to get in their strokes, the hospital staff became wholly demoralized, even though the attack was proceeding in the opposite direction. Wierzbowski and his men disarmed them and captured the hospital. Those Germans who were not directly serving the wounded were taken along as prisoners when the group escaped to American ground.

So finally they owed nothing to Regiment. They had pulled their getaway under their own power. That made it all the more remarkable that this small but valiant band returned to arms greatly depressed by a feeling that they had failed. They felt badly because they hadn't taken the bridge. They were ashamed that some of their comrades had run in panic the first night. They were downcast because they had been prisoners for a few hours.

Having known them all and worked among them, I can think of no better ending to the story than that beautiful line written by Elliot Paul: "It was a privilege to be associated with such courageous men and their enemies will do well to be afraid of them so long as they are above ground."

FIRST WAVE AT OMAHA BEACH

While the Mortars Fired

ALTHOUGH I had been for a brief time with the 29th Infantry Division at the battle of St.-Lô and discussed there with its commander, Major General Charlie Gerhardt, some part of the story of June 6, it was not until this division was in the lines and wholly engaged during the Siege of Brest that I completed the field work essential to determining what had happened to Gerhardt's troops at Omaha Beach.

That meant that the basic information concerning an operation in the late spring was not collected until late August. The units which had made the landing had in the interim fought their way from the eastern shore of the Cotentin almost to the extreme tip of Britanny. The outlook for this self-assignment was therefore anything but a happy one; too much time had passed. But the responsibility for the lag must be laid wholly to the inexcusable negligence of some of my fellow officers in the ETO Historical Division. Their shortcoming was that they would not work with troops if it meant dealing with front line danger, and since I was but an attached officer from the War Department general staff, with no authority over them, there was no way that I could hold their feet to the fire. Given my choice, I would have relieved or reclassified every officer who was derelict in this matter, though it was probably not necessary to go that far. If a commander keeps boring up to the battle, his subordinates quickly get the idea that if they hold back, they will shortly be in trouble. But an attached officer has little or no chance to move them by his example, and this is one of the problems besetting the role.

By the time I got to 29th Division, doing so because others had defaulted, I had already covered the two airborne divisions while in Normandy, dealt with First Infantry Division while it was in lines following the Breakout, and then trailed along with the Fourth Infantry Division through the Compiègne Forest and passed Mézières, compiling the data on their Utah Beach operation as we moved along. It was while on this latter stretch one day that one of the loonier incidents in a combat historian's life took place. Our enemy was at that time fading back rapidly and we rarely knew at any moment where the front lay, how far in front of us were German forces, or for that matter where our own flanks rested. I sat at a table questioning a group of NCO's from the 8th Infantry Regiment. Suddenly from behind a bush right at my back popped five German infantrymen with their hands raised. These were the only prisoners I captured in Europe. At that moment we were all of three miles behind our own front and those of us present felt disposed to reward the enemy with a bottle of beer apiece for being such nice boys.

The scene when I arrived in our lines outside Brest was quite different. The countryside is much like Normandy, fitted with even more formidable hedgerows and deeply sunken roads. So twisted were the opposing lines during the siege and such was the juxtaposition of them that one might stray from our own trenches into German country without having the slightest awareness of it. In fact, several hundred Americans became enemy prisoners during the siege merely from making a slight error in direction.

When I got to the command post of the 116th Regiment, the commander was anything but receptive. That was only partly because he was worn down by battle. He thought my mission was a sheer waste of time. He said to me: "Don't you realize that the regiment which fought at Omaha no longer exists? I'm talking about the people. We've been replaced wholly. The June 6th men are all either dead, in a hospital, missing or gone to other outfits as replacements." Then he added: "Isn't that so, Sergeant Major?" The NCO gravely nodded.

I said: "Colonel, all through this war I have been getting that story from other commanders, speaking of their platoons, companies or battalions. I have yet to experience the time when the story is true. There are always a few men who have come all the way through. You simply lose track of them. As long as there are a few I can get my work done. You let me have the Sergeant Major for a little while and we'll round up the survivors. Now I'm willing to bet you a hundred dollars that I'm right and you're dead wrong."

That took the wind out of his sails and we got started with the 116th Regiment. The result was as I had said it would be. The smallest number of survivors in any company was twelve, the largest was forty-seven.

In the commander of the First Battalion I met a kindred spirit, Major Tom Dallas, whose virtues as an officer I have elsewhere repeatedly extolled, as in *Men Against Fire*. I worked with his troops under fire on repeated occasions as, for example, when they were preparing to storm Fort Kergonant. But it is always true that assembly to hold a critique is more difficult during battle than when troops are in a resting situation; the work goes more slowly, breakoffs, because other requirements are imposed on the unit, are more frequent, and the interrogator is pressed harder to keep men concentrating on the object at hand. Thus it happened that after dealing with Dallas' Battalion half a dozen times at Brest I still had not completed the Omaha notes.

So we get to the last day of the battle. Dallas and Battalion had drawn the conclusive assignment. They were to storm the fields beyond Fort Montbarey, the rebuilt Napoleonic work which was the final enemy bastion short of the submarine pens. They had captured the fort the day before. When we got the entrenched fields beyond, we would have the city, and that terrible Nazi oaf, General Ramcke, would be on his way to a prison camp.

Dallas and outfit were already deployed at our extreme forward position and were due to jump off at 1300. The enemy's main works were approximately 450 yards ahead of the Battalion and the middle ground was flat all the way. These plans had been set the prior evening. But I was distressed by the fact that we had already lost a few of the Omaha survivors during the Brest Siege operations, which raised the possibility that more of the key figures would be eliminated in the charge against the fields of Montbarey. So I talked it over with Dallas and he agreed that we would hold a formation for my purposes in the front line beginning at 1100 of that day.

Lieutenant John G. Westover, my personal assistant, was with me, helping with the interrogations and serving as my jeep driver. The way to the Battalion was along a sunken road which in fact described Dallas' front. That is to say that the men were waiting behind the giant hedgerow on one side of the road while no man's land extended toward the Germans from the other side of it.

When we got within 500 yards of the Battalion the sunken road was a slot of fire from end to end. The German mortars were seeking the Battalion, the enemy knowing that the attack was coming, but the shells were all breaking along the road just short of the men. I had chosen Westover as my assistant because he is one of the guttiest officers that I have ever known. So when he stopped the jeep just short of the curtain of shells, there was good reason.

I asked John: "Why are you stopping?"

He said: "You know it doesn't make sense to run that fire. We won't get there."

I said: "John, you are probably right. It looks very fool-

ish, but when once you hold back in combat from doing what
you are obligated to do then it becomes easier to do the
same thing ever after. We bound ourselves to meet with
this Battalion."

He yelled: "Then let's go!" He gave the jeep the gun and
we got through without a scratch.

But joining up with Dallas, we still had a problem of
how to proceed. Clearly there was every reason to expect
that the shelling would continue until jumpoff time. To
expose the Battalion to fire just prior to an assault would
be unthinkable.

But we had awaiting us a tailor-made situation. The men
were all huddled or rather strung out in line right next
the protecting hedgerow; about thirty yards to the rear of it
was a concrete cistern just deep enough for a man standing
therein to pop his head above the rim. It was a stage setting
ideally suited to solve the problem. We left the men where

The Cistern and Field at Brest

they were already disposed. Dallas and his staff officers got into the cistern. Westover and I held forth in the open ground midway between them. The boom-boom continued right through the two hours and we had to shout at top voice to make ourselves understood. An occasional shell came over the embankment and broke in our field though there were no truly close ones. I stood and yelled out the questions. Westover sat and wrote down the minutes as I dictated them. The men all concentrated on the work. It was one of the most productive critiques in my memory and by the end of it we had at long last completed the Omaha story.

This was not a unique experience. But of all the critiques which were conducted under fire I think that the circumstances of this one were most bizarre and the necessitousness was near absolute. But to quote another of my officers, Lieutenant Fred Hadsel, after he had experimented in the historical coverage of armored operations by riding a tank during an attack: "It is not a method which is recommended for SOP because the interrogator may not survive his experience and a dead historian can write little better than most of the live ones I know." Amen!

First Wave at Omaha Beach

UNLIKE what happens to other great battles, the passing of the years and the retelling of the story have softened the horror of Omaha Beach on D Day.

This fluke of history is doubly ironic since no other decisive battle has ever been so thoroughly reported for the official record. While the troops were still fighting in Western France, what had happened to each unit in the Normandy landing had become known through the eyewitness testimony of all survivors. It was this research by the field historians which first determined where each company had hit the beach and by what route it had moved inland. Owing to the fact that every unit save one had been mislanded, it took this work to show the troops where they had fought.

How they fought and what they suffered were also determined in detail during the field research. As published today, the map data showing where the troops came ashore check exactly with the work done in the field; but the accompanying narrative describing their ordeal is a sanitized version of the original field notes.

This happened because the Army historians who wrote the first official book about Omaha Beach, basing it on the field notes, did a calculated job of sifting and weighting the material. So saying does not imply that their judgment was wrong. Normandy was an American victory; it was their duty to trace the twists and turns of fortune by which success was won. But to follow that rule slights the story of

Omaha as an epic human tragedy which in the early hours bordered on total disaster. On this two-division front landing, only six rifle companies were relatively effective as units. They did better than others mainly because they had the luck to touch down on a less deadly section of the beach. Three times that number were shattered or foundered before they could start to fight. Several contributed not a man or a bullet to the battle for the high ground. But their ordeal has gone unmarked because its detail was largely ignored by history in the first place. The worst-fated companies were overlooked, the more wretched personal experiences were toned down, and disproportionate attention was paid to the little element of courageous success in a situation which was largely characterized by tragic failure.

The official accounts which came later took their cue from this secondary source instead of searching the original documents. Even such an otherwise splendid and popular book on the great adventure as Cornelius Ryan's *The Longest Day* misses the essence of the Omaha story.

In everything that has been written about Omaha until now, there is less blood and iron than in the original field notes covering any battalion landing in the first wave. Doubt it? Then let's follow along with Able and Baker Companies, 116th Infantry, 29th Division. Their story is lifted from my fading Normandy notebook, which covers the landing of every Omaha company.

Able Company riding the tide in seven Higgins boats is still five thousand yards from the beach when first taken under artillery fire. The shells fall short. At one thousand yards, Boat No. 5 is hit dead on and founders. Six men drown before help arrives. Second Lieutenant Edward Gearing and twenty others paddle around until picked up by naval craft, thereby missing the fight at the shore line. It's their lucky day. The other six boats ride unscathed to within one hundred yards of the shore, where a shell into Boat

No. 3 kills two men. Another dozen drown, taking to the water as the boat sinks. That leaves five boats.

Lieutenant Edward Tidrick in Boat No. 2 cries out: "My God, we're coming in at the right spot, but look at it! No shingle, no wall, no shell holes, no cover. Nothing!" His men are at the sides of the boat, straining for a view of the target. They stare but say nothing. At exactly 6:36 A.M. ramps are dropped along the boat line and the men jump off in water anywhere from waist deep to higher than a man's head. This is the signal awaited by the Germans atop the bluff. Already pounded by mortars, the floundering line is instantly swept by crossing machine-gun fires from both ends of the beach.

Able Company has planned to wade ashore in three files from each boat, center file going first, then flank files peeling off to right and left. The first men out try to do this but are ripped apart before they can make five yards. Even the lightly wounded die by drowning, doomed by the water-logging of their overloaded packs. From Boat No. 1, all hands jump off in water over their heads. Most of them are carried down. Ten or so survivors get around the boat and clutch at its sides in an attempt to stay afloat. The same thing happens to the section in Boat No. 4. Half of its people are lost to the fire or tide before anyone gets ashore. All order has vanished from Able Company before it has fired a shot.

Already the sea runs red. Even among some of the lightly wounded who jump into shallow water the hits prove fatal. Knocked down by a bullet in the arm or weakened by fear and shock, they are unable to rise again and are drowned by the onrushing tide. Other wounded men drag themselves ashore and, on finding the sands, lie quiet from total exhaustion, only to be overtaken and killed by the water. A few move safely through the bullet swarm to the beach, then find that they cannot hold there. They return to the water to use it for body cover. Faces turned upward, so that their nostrils are out of water, they creep toward the land at the same rate as the tide. That is how most of the survivors make it. The less rugged or less clever seek the cover of enemy obstacles moored along the upper half of the beach and are knocked off by machine-gun fire.

Within seven minutes after the ramps drop, Able Company is inert and leaderless. At Boat No. 2, Lieutenant Tidrick takes a bullet through the throat as he jumps from the ramp into the water. He staggers onto the sand and flops down ten feet from Private First Class Leo J. Nash. Nash sees the blood spurting and hears the strangled words gasped by Tidrick: "Advance with the wire cutters!" It's futile; Nash has no cutters. To give the order, Tidrick has raised himself up on his hands and made himself a target for an instant. Nash, burrowing into the sand, sees machine-gun bullets rip Tidrick from crown to pelvis. From the cliff above, the German gunners are shooting into the survivors as from a roof top.

Captain Taylor N. Fellers and Lieutenant Benjamin R. Kearfoot never make it. They had loaded with a section of thirty men in Boat No. 6 (Landing Craft, Assault, No. 1015). But exactly what happened to this boat and its human cargo is never to be known. No one saw the craft go down. How each man aboard it met death remains unreported. Half of the drowned bodies were later found along the beach. It is supposed that the others were claimed by the sea.

Along the beach, only one Able Company officer still lives —Lieutenant Elijah Nance, who is hit in the heel as he quits the boat and hit in the belly by a second bullet as he makes the sand. By the end of ten minutes, every sergeant is either dead or wounded. To the eyes of such men as Gilbert G. Murdock, this clean sweep suggests that the Germans on the high ground have spotted all leaders and concentrated fire their way. Among the men who are still moving in with the tide, rifles, packs, and helmets have already been cast away in the interests of survival.

To the right of where Tidrick's boat is drifting with the tide, its coxswain lying dead next to the shell-shattered wheel, the seventh craft, carrying a medical section with one officer and sixteen men, noses toward the beach. The ramp drops. In that instant, two machine guns concentrate their fire on the opening. Not a man is given time to jump. All aboard are cut down where they stand.

By the end of fifteen minutes, Able Company has still not fired a weapon. No orders are being given by anyone. No words are spoken. The few able-bodied survivors move or not as they see fit. Merely to stay alive is a full-time job. The fight has become a rescue operation in which nothing counts but the force of a strong example.

Above all others stands out the first-aid man, Thomas Breedin. Reaching the sands, he strips off pack, blouse, helmet, and boots. For a moment he stands there so that others on the strand will see him and get the same idea. Then he crawls into the water to pull in wounded men about to be overlapped by the tide. The deeper water is still spotted with tide walkers advancing at the same pace as the rising water. But now, owing to Breedin's example, the strongest among them become more conspicuous targets. Coming along, they pick up wounded comrades and float them to the shore raftwise. Machine-gun fire still rakes the water. Burst after burst spoils the rescue act, shooting the floating man from the hands of the walker or killing both together. But Breedin for this hour leads a charmed life and stays with his work indomitably.

By the end of one half-hour, approximately two-thirds of the company is forever gone. There is no precise casualty figure for that moment. There is for the Normandy landing as a whole no accurate figure for the first hour or first day. The circumstances precluded it. Whether more Able Company riflemen died from water than from fire is known only to heaven. All earthly evidence so indicates, but cannot prove it.

By the end of one hour, the survivors from the main body have crawled across the sand to the foot of the bluff, where there is a narrow sanctuary of defiladed space. There they lie all day, clean spent, unarmed, too shocked to feel hunger, incapable even of talking to one another. No one happens by to succor them, ask what has happened, provide water, or offer unwanted pity. D Day at Omaha afforded no time or space for such missions. Every landing company was overloaded by its own assault problems.

By the end of one hour and forty-five minutes, six survivors from the boat section on the extreme right shake loose and work their way to a shelf a few rods up the cliff. Four fall exhausted from the short climb and advance no farther. They stay there through the day, seeing no one else from the company. The other two, Privates Jake Shefer and Thomas Lovejoy, join a group from the Second Ranger Battalion, which is assaulting Pointe du Hoe to the right of the company sector, and fight on with the Rangers through the day. Two men. Two rifles. Except for these, Able Company's contribution to the D-Day fire fight is a cipher.

Baker company, which is scheduled to land twenty-six minutes after Able and right on top of it, supporting and reinforcing, has its full load of trouble on the way in. So rough is the sea during the journey that the men have to bail furiously with their helmets to keep the six boats from swamping. Thus preoccupied, they do not see the disaster which is overtaking Able until they are almost atop it. Then, what their eyes behold is either so limited or so staggering to the senses that control withers, the assault wave begins to dissolve, and disunity induced by fear virtually cancels the mission. A great cloud of smoke and dust raised by the mortar and machine-gun fire has almost closed a curtain around Able Company's ordeal. Outside the pall, nothing is to be seen but a line of corpses adrift, a few heads bobbing in the water and the crimson-running tide. But this is enough for the British coxswains. They raise the cry: "We can't go in there. We can't see the landmarks. We must pull off."

In the command boat, Captain Ettore V. Zappacosta pulls a Colt .45 and says: "By God, you'll take this boat straight in." His display of courage wins obedience, but it's still a fool's order. Such of Baker's boats as try to go straight in suffer Able's fate without helping the other company whatever. Thrice during the approach mortar shells break right next to Zappacosta's boat but by an irony leave it unscathed, thereby sparing the riders a few more moments of life. At seventy-five yards from the sand Zappacosta yells: "Drop the ramp!" The end goes down, and a storm of bullet fire comes in.

Zappacosta jumps first from the boat, reels ten yards through the elbow-high tide, and yells back: "I'm hit." He staggers on a few more steps. The aid man, Thomas Kenser, sees him bleeding from hip and shoulder. Kenser yells: "Try to make it in; I'm coming." But the captain falls face forward into the wave, and the weight of his equipment and soaked pack pin him to the bottom. Kenser jumps toward him and is shot dead while in the air. Lieutenant Tom Dallas of Charley Company, who has come along to make a reconnaissance, is the third man. He makes it to the edge of the sand. There a machine-gun burst blows his head apart before he can flatten.

Private First Class Robert L. Sales, who is lugging Zappacosta's radio (an SCR 300), is the fourth man to leave the boat, having waited long enough to see the others die. His boot heel catches on the edge of the ramp and he falls sprawling into the tide, losing the radio but saving his life. Every man who tries to follow him is either killed or wounded before reaching dry land. Sales alone gets to the beach unhit. To travel those few yards takes him two hours. First he crouches in the water, and waddling forward on his haunches just a few paces, collides with a floating log—driftwood. In that moment, a mortar shell explodes just above his head, knocking him groggy. He hugs the log to keep from going down, and somehow the effort seems to clear his head a little. Next thing he knows, one of Able Company's tide walkers hoists him aboard the log and, using his sheath knife, cuts away Sales's pack, boots, and assault jacket.

Feeling stronger, Sales returns to the water, and from behind the log, using it as cover, pushes toward the sand. Private Mack L. Smith of Baker Company, hit three times through the face, joins him there. An Able Company rifleman named Kemper, hit thrice in the right leg, also comes alongside. Together they follow the log until at last they roll it to the farthest reach of high tide. Then they flatten themselves behind it, staying there for hours after the flow has turned to ebb. The dead of both companies wash up to where they lie, and then wash back out to sea again. As a body drifts in close to them, Sales and companions, disregarding the fire, crawl from behind the log to take a look. If any one of them recognizes the face of a comrade, they join in dragging the body up onto the dry sand beyond the water's reach. The unfamiliar dead are left to the sea. So long as the tide is full, they stay at this task. Later, an unidentified first-aid man who comes wiggling along the beach dresses the wounds of Smith. Sales, as he finds strength, bandages Kemper. The three remain behind the log until night falls. There is nothing else to be reported of any member of Zappacosta's boat team.

Only one other Baker Company boat tries to come straight in to the beach. Somehow the boat founders. Somehow all of its people are killed—one British coxswain and about thirty American infantrymen. Where they fall, there is no one to take note and report.

Frightened coxswains in the other four craft take one quick look, instinctively draw back, and then veer right and left away from the Able Company shambles. So doing, they dodge their duty while giving a break to their passen-

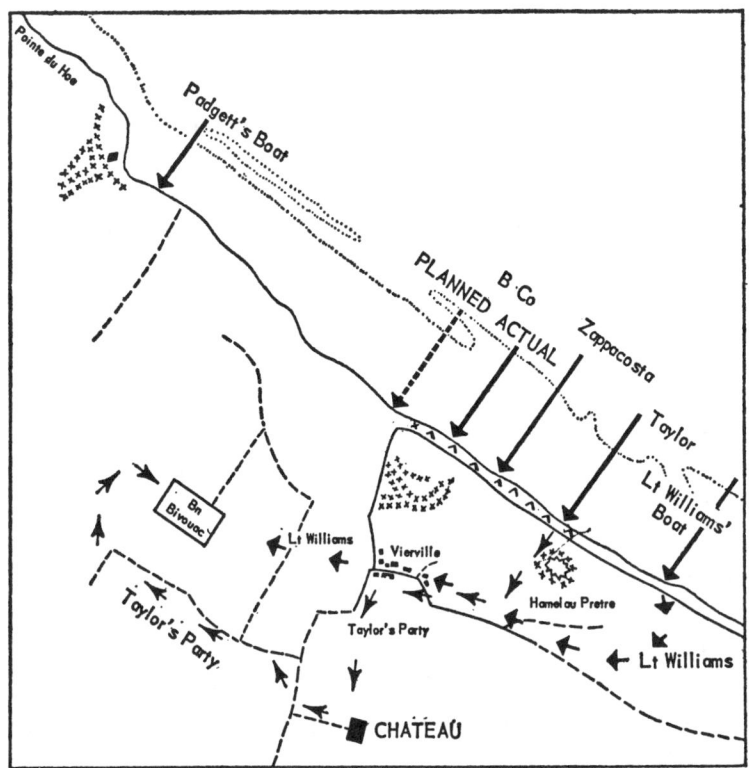

The Landings at Vierville

gers. Such is the shock to the boat team leaders, and such their feeling of relief at the turning movement, that not one utters a protest. Lieutenant Leo A. Pingenot's coxswain swings the boat far rightward toward Pointe du Hoe; then, spying a small and deceptively peaceful-looking cove, heads directly for the land. Fifty yards out, Pingenot yells: "Drop the ramp!" The coxswain freezes on the rope, refusing to lower. Staff Sergeant Odell L. Padgett jumps him, throttles him, and bears him to the floor. Padgett's men lower the rope and jump for the water. In two minutes they are all in up to their necks and struggling to avoid drowning. That quickly, Pingenot is already far out ahead of them. Padgett comes even with him, and together they cross onto dry land. The beach of the cove is heavily strewn with giant boulders. Bullets seem to be pinging off every rock.

Pingenot and Padgett dive behind the same rock. Then they glance back, but to their horror see not one person. Quite suddenly smoke has half blanked out the scene beyond the water's edge. Pingenot moans: "My God, the whole boat team is dead." Padgett sings out: "Hey, are you hit?" Back come many voices from beyond the smoke. "What's the rush?" "Take it easy!" "We'll get there." "Where's the fire?" "Who wants to know?" The men are still moving along, using the water as cover. Padgett's yell is their first information that anyone else has moved up front. They all make it to the shore, and they are twenty-eight strong at first. Pingenot and Padgett manage to stay ahead of them, coaxing and encouraging. Padgett keeps yelling: "Come on, goddamn it, things are better up there!" But still they lose two men killed and three wounded in crossing the beach.

In the cove, the Platoon latches on to a company of Rangers, fights all day as part of that company, and helps destroy the enemy entrenchments atop Pointe du Hoe. By sundown that mop-up is completed. The Platoon bivouacs at the first hedgerow beyond the cliff.

Another Baker Company boat, which turns to the right, has far less luck. Staff Sergeant Robert M. Campbell, who leads the section, is the first man to jump out when the ramp goes down. He drops in drowning water, and his load of two bangalore torpedoes takes him straight to the bottom. So he jettisons the bangalores and then, surfacing, cuts away all equipment for good measure. Machine-gun fire brackets him, and he submerges again briefly. Never a strong swimmer, he heads back out to sea. For two hours he paddles around, two hundred or so yards from the shore. Though he hears and sees nothing of the battle, he somehow gets the impression that the invasion has failed and that all other

Americans are dead, wounded, or have been taken prisoner. Strength fast going, in despair he moves ashore rather than drown. Beyond the smoke he quickly finds the fire. So he grabs a helmet from a dead man's head, crawls on hands and knees to the sea wall, and there finds five of his men, two of them unwounded.

Like Campbell, Private First Class Jan J. Budziszewski is carried to the bottom by his load of two bangalores. He hugs them half a minute before realizing that he will either let loose or drown. Next, he shucks off his helmet and pack and drops his rifle. Then he surfaces. After swimming 200 yards, he sees that he is moving in exactly the wrong direction. So he turns about and heads for the beach, where he crawls ashore "under a rain of bullets." In his path lies a dead Ranger. Budziszewski takes the dead man's helmet, rifle, and canteen and crawls on to the sea wall. The only survivor from Campbell's boat section to get off the beach, he spends his day walking to and fro along the foot of the bluff, looking for a friendly face. But he meets only strangers, and none shows any interest in him.

In Lieutenant William B. Williams' boat, the coxswain steers sharp left and away from Zappacosta's sector. Not seeing the Captain die, Williams doesn't know that command has now passed to him. Guiding on his own instinct, the coxswain moves along the coast six hundred yards, then puts the boat straight in. It's a good guess; he has found a little vacuum in the battle. The ramp drops on dry sand and the boat team jumps ashore. Yet it's a close thing. Mortar fire has dogged them all the way; and as the last rifleman clears the ramp, one shell lands dead center of the boat, blows it apart, and kills the coxswain. Momentarily, the beach is free of fire, but the men cannot cross it at a bound. Weak from seasickness and fear, they move at a crawl, dragging their equipment. By the end of twenty minutes, Williams and ten men are over the sand and resting in the lee of the sea wall. Five others are hit by machine-gun fire crossing the beach;

six men, last seen while taking cover in a tidal pocket, are never heard from again. More mortar fire lands around the party as Williams leads it across the road beyond the sea wall. The men scatter. When the shelling lifts, three of them do not return. Williams leads the seven survivors up a trail toward the fortified village of Les Moulins atop the bluff. He recognizes the ground and knows that he is taking on a tough target. Les Moulins is perched above a draw, up which winds a dirt road from the beach, designated on the invasion maps as Exit No. 3.

Strong Point Attacked by Williams

Williams and his crew of seven are the first Americans to approach it D-Day morning. Machine-gun fire from a concrete pillbox sweeps over them as they near the brow of the hill, moving now at a crawl through thick grass. Williams says to the others: "Stay here; we're too big a target!" They hug earth, and he crawls forward alone, moving via a shallow gully. Without being detected, he gets to within twenty yards of the gun, obliquely downslope from it. He heaves a grenade; but he has held it just a bit too long and it explodes in air, just outside the embrasure. His second grenade hits the concrete wall and bounces right back on him. Three of its slugs hit him in the shoulders. Then, from out of the pillbox, a German potato masher sails down on him and explodes just a few feet away; five more fragments cut into him. He starts crawling back to his men; en route, three bullets from the machine gun rip his rump and right leg.

The seven are still there. Williams hands his map and compass to Staff Sergeant Frank M. Price, saying: "It's your job now. But go the other way—toward Vierville." Price starts to look at Williams' wounds, but Williams shakes him off, saying: "No, get moving." He then settles himself in a hole in the embankment, stays there all day, and at last gets medical attention just before midnight.

On leaving Williams, Price's first act is to hand map and compass (the symbols of leadership) to Technical Sergeant William Pearce, whose seniority the Lieutenant has overlooked. They cross the draw, one man at a time, and some distance beyond come to a ravine; on the far side, they bump their first hedgerow, and as they look for an entrance, fire comes against them. Behind a second hedgerow, not more than thirty yards away, are seven Germans, five rifles and two burp guns. On exactly even terms, these two forces engage for the better part of an hour, apparently with no one's getting hit. Then Pearce settles the fight by crawling along a drainage ditch to the enemy flank. He kills the seven Germans with a Browning Automatic Rifle.

For Pearce and his friends, it is a first taste of battle; its success is giddying. Heads up, they walk along the road straight into Vierville, disregarding all precautions. They get away with it only because that village is already firmly in the hands of Lieutenant Walter Taylor of Baker Company and twenty men from his boat team.

Taylor is a luminous figure in the story of D Day, one of the forty-seven immortals of Omaha who, by their dauntless initiative at widely separated points along the beach, saved the landing from total stagnation and disaster. Courage and luck are his in extraordinary measure.

When Baker Company's assault wave breaks up just short of the surf where Able Company is in ordeal, Taylor's coxswain swings his boat sharp left, then heads toward the shore about halfway between Zappacosta's boat and Williams'. Until a few seconds after the ramp drops, this bit of beach next to the village called Hamel-au-Prêtre is blessedly clear of fire. No mortar shells crown the start. Taylor leads his section crawling across the beach and over the sea wall, losing four men killed and two wounded (machine-gun fire) in this brief movement. Some yards off to his right, Taylor has seen Lieutenants Harold Donaldson and Emil Winkler shot dead. But there is no halt for reflection; Taylor leads the section by trail straight up the bluff and into Vierville, where his luck continues. In a two-hour fight he whips a German platoon without losing a man.

The village is quiet when Pearce joins him. Pearce says: "Williams is shot up back there and can't move."

Says Taylor: "I guess that makes me company commander."

Answers Pearce: "This is probably all of Baker Company." Pearce takes a head count; they number twenty-eight, including Taylor.

Says Taylor: "That ought to be enough. Follow me!"

Inland from Vierville about 500 yards lies the Château de Vaumicel, imposing in its rock-walled massiveness, its hedgerow-bordered fields all entrenched and interconnected with artilleryproof tunnels. To every man but Taylor the target looks prohibitive. Still, they follow him. Fire stops them one hundred yards short of the château. The Germans are behind a hedgerow at mid-distance. Still feeling their way, Taylor's men flatten, open fire with rifles, and toss a few grenades, though the distance seems too great. By sheer chance, one grenade glances off the helmet of a German squatting in a foxhole. He jumps up, shouting; *"Kamerad! Kamerad!"* Thereupon twenty-four of the enemy walk from behind the hedgerow with their hands in the air. Taylor pares off one of his riflemen to march the prisoners back to the beach. The brief fight cost him three wounded. Within the château, he takes two more prisoners, a German doctor and his first-aid man. Taylor puts them on a "kind of a parole," leaving his three wounded in their keeping while moving his platoon to the first crossroads beyond the château.

Here he is stopped by the sudden arrival of three truck-loads of German infantry, who deploy into the fields on both flanks of his position and start an envelopment. The manpower odds, about three to one against him, are too heavy. In the first trade of fire, lasting not more than two minutes, a rifleman lying beside Taylor is killed, three others are wounded, and the BAR is shot from Pearce's hands. That leaves but twenty men and no automatic weapons.

Taylor yells: "Back to the château!" They go out, crawling as far as the first hedgerow; then they rise and trot along, supporting their wounded. Taylor is the last man out, having stayed behind to cover the withdrawl with his carbine until the hedgerows interdict fire against the others. So far, the small group has had no contact with any other part of the expedition, and for all its members know, the invasion may have failed.

They make it to the château. The enemy comes on and moves in close. The attacking fire builds up. But the stone walls are fire-slotted, and through the midday and early afternoon these ports well serve the American riflemen. The question is whether the ammunition will outlast the Germans. It is answered at sundown, just as the supply runs out, by the arrival of fifteen Rangers who join their fire with Taylor's, and the Germans fade back.

Already Taylor and his force are farther south than any element of the right flank in the Omaha expedition. But Taylor isn't satisfied. The Battalion objective, as specified for the close of D Day, is still more than one-half mile to the westward. He says to the others: "We've got to make it."

So he leads them forth, once again serving as first scout, eighteen of his own riflemen and fifteen Rangers following in column. One man is killed by a bullet getting away from Vaumicel. Dark closes over them. They prepare to bivouac. Having got almost to the village of Louviers, they are by this time almost one-half mile in front of anything else in the United States Army. There a runner reaches them with the message that the remnants of the Battalion are assembling seven hundred yards closer to the sea; Taylor and party are directed to fall back on them. It is done.

Later, still under the spell, Price paid the perfect tribute to Taylor. He said: "We saw no sign of fear in him. Watching him made men of us. Marching or fighting, he was leading. We followed him because there was nothing else to do."

Thousands of Americans were spilled onto Omaha Beach. The high ground was won by a handful of men like Taylor who on that day burned with a flame bright beyond common understanding.

"FIX BAYONETS AND
FOLLOW ME!"

About Operation Punch

By January 20, 1951, the Chinese Communist Army was as far south of Seoul as it was ever going to get. Before it ever crossed the Han River, it was already overextended and gasping for supply. Its logistical straitjacket could not be shaken off because of the great distance to the Yalu, the wretched condition of the iced-over roads and our command of the air. All of this was fully predictable out of what we had learned of their rate of movement, their supply system and communications difficulties, etc. while we were still retreating out of North Korea. I maintained then with my superiors, and I maintain now, that we could have stopped them in front of Seoul and that we should have prepared to fight a decisive battle in defense of the ROK capital. But no one who had the power was willing to make the decision in time. So once again the heart of free Korea got sacked by the enemy.

I think it was on January 18 that I returned briefly to the Army headquarters in Taegu, following a bout with pneumonia which struck me down while I was in the field with the 1st Marine Division. General Matthew B. Ridgway had but recently taken over the command and was already forward with his divisions, exerting his personal influence to buck up their combat morale. All along the line the 8th Army was at a standstill, having reached the limit of its recoil and being virtually out of contact with the enemy. The question in all minds was what we would do next. My friends on the General Staff could afford me no light; they didn't know in what sector we would first attempt a recovery. In such circumstances one has to guide on instinct if one is to get to the critical area in time. By looking at the war room maps in Taegu, I judged that we would have to hit first out of Suwon and that the U.S. I Corps would deal the first blow. The wish may have been father to the thought, since I wanted to see more of that doughty warrior, Lieutenant General "Shrimp" Milburn, the best corps commander in Korea. At my request orders were so written. When I got to the airport I found a note from my clerk-typist, Sergeant Shafer, informing me that he had been so badly overworked in the field that he was turning into the hospital with a lame wrist. I never saw him again and from that time forward I had to do all of my own field clerical work. We took off on a foggy, foggy morning; on no other air trip in my life have I seen so many rocks pop up right at hand within the clouds.

At I Corps, Milburn steered me to headquarters of the 25th Infantry Division and from there to the CP of the 27th Wolfhound Regiment. All three of these headquarters were grouped close together within Suwon. It was in this way that I chanced to move in with an old friend, Colonel John Hershey Michaelis, commander of the Wolfhounds.

My hunch had been right. Something was afoot. Preparation for battle was already well under way and the 27th Regiment was scheduled for a pivotal part. The story of Operation Punch and the attack on Hill 440 is told elsewhere. In the days that immediately followed my joining Michaelis I was called in to consult on the tactics for that highly successful operation, mathematically the slickest show staged in any of our recent wars. The advance was to be staged by armored columns hitting in combination with infantry battalions. My part of it was to advise on how the command structure should be regulated so that it would have unity no matter what we ran up against. Twice within recent weeks U.S. forces had been trapped and mangled in fire gauntlets rigged by the Chinese along the high ground dominating main supply routes. We wanted to be sure that this would never happen again. In Operation Punch we went to a radical solution on how command responsibility was to be placed and shifted according to the way the battle developed, and it worked like a charm.

While I was first with the Wolfhounds my attention was drawn to Easy Company because of the peculiarly aggressive character of its new commander, Captain Lewis Millett, who had recently shifted over from artillery at his own request. Such a change is so unusual that I wanted to see the man. To describe Lew at that stage in one word, he bristled. He was taking in utmost seriousness Ridgway's stricture that all of his infantrymen should take to the bayonet and prepare to close with the enemy. Lew was giving his men a straight eight hours a day of hardening with this weapon, which is approximately the rigor in an advanced bayonet school where instructors are conditioned. Since I had gone this course of sprouts in the first AEF, I relished the opportunity to watch him work. There was no doubt that Millett knew the full routine. But he had eliminated all the frills such as butt strokes and neck chops and was concentrating exclusively on the killing strokes—the long point and the short point. A hard taskmaster, he was demanding precision of his men in these few things which he thought counted most. I remarked to him one day: "Captain Millett, you can try till hell freezes over and it won't make much difference anyway. When men become so overwrought that they close with the bayonet, they forget everything they have been taught and do whatever comes easiest; it becomes a rough and tumble, a melee; you'll see no long points executed if your men ever charge with cold steel."

When Operation Punch rolled, I was first with Task Force Bartlett, the armor-infantry column on the left flank, hitting via the main highway which runs from Suwon toward

Inchon. And well I remember the day because of one incident which repeated what I had twice experienced in
earlier wars. The Task Force CP was about one-half mile
off the main highway across paddy fields which were too
thinly iced for passage by a jeep. So I took off afoot across
the stretch with not another person in sight. Halfway, three
mortar shells came in, exploding within fifty or so yards of
me. The terror I knew was almost overwhelming. I ran
until I was exhausted. It always happens that way. Be a
man ever so accustomed to fire, experiencing it when he is
alone and unobserved produces shock that is indescribable.
Whether the difference comes of some atavistic fear or is
more truly a reflex of the purely selfish though human feeling that if one must die one should at least get public
credit for it is a question for the psychiatrists. I don't know
the answer, I only know what happens.

When Millett's first and second bayonet attacks were staged,
I was within viewing distance of the action. But it was not
possible to break off and devote my attention immediately
to this company. I was shuttling between Task Force Bartlett
and Task Force Dolvin, the armored column on the right
flank, doing this travel by helicopter. In such hours as were
left me I was going by jeep to the infantry battalions
attacking Hill 440, the massive ridge in the middle ground
which was the anchor of the whole enemy defense line. All
of these movements were necessary so that I could start
with a balanced view of the operation as a whole, from which
perspective I could better estimate what parts had to be
analyzed in detail. For example, while I knew day by day
what the infantry companies at Hill 440 were up against
and how they were faring, it wasn't until we got to the line of
the Han about one week later and they were guarding
our front at Yongdong-Po that I was able to critique their
small unit contributions.

However, in the case of Millett and his company there
was almost no delay. Because of Ridgway's accent on the

bayonet and awareness of what one shining example might do for the army as a whole if we got to it promptly, there was reason for urgency. On the first morning after the big charge at Anyang-Ni, we assembled the company. The big hill was right at hand. The critique was conducted in and around a tent not more than five hundred yards from its base. The company was then in a holding position, while the armor fought on northward and the issue at Hill 440 remained undecided. The critique lasted approximately six hours and there were no reluctant witnesses.

But I almost missed one item which came out near the end. They had told me everything, they said, and I had closed my notebook. Then I spoke up, saying something like this: "It's funny, I have only run into one other episode such as this where Americans in a fight go berserk and emotional control simply vanishes. That is what happened to you, you know. You all blew your lids. The other incident was Millsap's Patrol in the Normandy action. Its men got so steamed up that after killing the Germans they went on to slaughter the cattle and chickens around the farmhouse."

One Sergeant then spoke up rather sheepishly and said: "Colonel, we weren't going to tell you. That's what happened to us, you know. The geeks had a bunch of Mongolian ponies staked out on that hill. We slaughtered every last one of them."

"Fix Bayonets and Follow Me!"

IN the beginning, anyone might have said that Captain Lewis Millett's chance of putting his personal stamp on Easy Company of the 27th Infantry Wolfhounds was not too bright.

Easy Company was already a going enterprise, and knew it. Still under the spell of their late adored leader, Captain Reginald Desiderio, the men could remember with pride that they had matched him, courage for courage, in the last great fight which had cost his life.

That is a story which still must be told—a company action, desperate as any other in the terrible November battle along the Chongchon River.

Together, Captain Desiderio and his company had stood fast when the Chinese had caught them well forward of all other elements in the 25th Infantry Division with nothing on their flanks to thwart envelopment.

Through one unending night they were a tiny island of resistance in a sea of frenzied enemies. On their lonely hill, they met the shock head-on and held, Desiderio shouting to his men, "Hold till dawn and we've got it made!"—until they picked up the cry and it became a chant.

Death and wounds checked the words in many a throat before the promise came true. The Chinese paid tenfold for the bodies Easy carried from the hill and the walking wounded who hobbled back in the end under their own power.

Just after dawn the Chinese drew off—beaten on the local ground. That could have been a magic hour. But in their last wild charge, moments before, the enemy had cracked Easy's perimeter. Desiderio, seeing his line crumbling, started for the threatened point. A mortar shell, glancing from a tank, struck him down. The men saw the first light of morning reflected from their dead captain's face.

Higher authority took due note of these deeds. Easy Company was recommended for the Distinguished Unit Citation. Desiderio was put in for a posthumous Medal of Honor.

This was the command and tradition which Captain Lewis Millett chose to take over, hoping that he might give them a little lift. It was a very big order.

I met him while I was working with Easy, reconstructing the Desiderio fight. He stood on the sidelines as I interviewed the unit, listening hard, but saying nothing. It had not been his show. He left the leading of the critique to Lieutenant J. C. Burch, who had been with Desiderio. Easy Company was even then in process of moving from a blocking position into an attack.

There were other unusual things about Millett, signs that he was a little bit crazy—like a fox. For months he had been an outstanding forward observer with the 8th Field Artillery Battalion. Maybe it was a matter of wanting the name as well as the game. He asked for transfer to the Infantry. On 1 January he got his wish and Easy got its new skipper.

They saw a man who probably wouldn't stand out anywhere in a crowd except for a gorgeous mustache the color of ripe cornsilk and an eye that bores like a gimlet. And he is a man who moves about as if there were coiled springs in his shoepacs.

On taking over, he didn't turn Easy Company upside down. There were, however, a few modest changes in weapons.

He put two BAR's in each squad.

Then he started the practice of loading each man with four to six grenades. This departure was not an unqualified success. There is a natural resistance in an already burdened fighter to carrying more than two grenades, even when he knows he will be closely engaged. No discipline can wholly overcome it. Easy Company finally settled for something like this: Those who could carry more grenades did so. The average man continued to carry two. A resupply of about 150 grenades was kept in the ammo-jeep trailer. In each platoon, one man was put in charge of issuing grenades in order to prevent waste. Squad leaders were held accountable that every man would have a grenade load on entering combat.

But the main change was made in the bayonet.

Like most infantry companies in Korea, Easy had thrown that weapon away. Millett got a resupply. He put one on his own M1 and kept it there. All of his following were required to do likewise.

And back of the line, he gave the Company bayonet drill. Not much—only two days of two hours each. He cut the strokes down to the bare essentials, using only the long thrust (or point), short thrust, jab, and modified butt stroke.

But while the fatigue of standard drill was thus avoided, something extra was added. Millett made his men live with the bayonet, talk it, bed it, and eat it. When the Company moved, men had to have bayonets ready. Afield, they'd be thrown into bayonet charges against stacks of rice straw. On the march, they'd have a go at a mud bank. Whatever was stickable was stuck. Day by day the men got muscled to swinging a rifle with a bayonet fixed.

Millett said, and kept repeating: "In our next fight, we'll use this. Have it ready!"

This brought one particularly vexing problem. The issue bayonet is too dull to cut butter. The men asked for whetstones. The Army didn't seem to have any. So the men took their problem to the housewives of the Korean neighborhood. Bayonets were sharpened on crude stones from Korean kitchens. The result was something less than a razor edge.

This was about the size of it up to the time of Operation Punch, the perfectly coordinated armor-and-infantry attack which, in early February, 1951, carried I Corps from Suwon to the Han River, opened the door to Seoul, and marked the real beginning of the American recovery.

Easy Company's fight under Millett was only one small piece of the general engagement fought by the 25th Infantry Division, with the 3d Infantry Division doing a noble job on its right.

From Suwon, two roads, approximately 6000 meters apart, run to the Han, which is about twenty-five miles north of the city. Both roads are enfiladed by successive ridgelines running approximately at right angles to them all the way to the river.

Seven miles out of Suwon, in the middle ground, is Hill 440. By any sensible standard, it should be called a mountain. It is almost sheer rock, a complex of palisaded ridges with cliff facings of such abruptness that only an alpinist would undertake to climb them frontally. Gibraltar itself does not look more formidable.

Hill 440 dominates the whole countryside. Beyond it the ridges are lower and fall off more gently toward the river. The enemy had figured it out right and had bunkered in on 440's skyline in great strength. While that key position was held, there could be no moving on the two roads to punish the enemy flanks. The crown of 440 was ice-covered; the night temperatures were only a few degrees above zero. The Turks had a go at 440 and were worsted. Then, as February opened, the Second Battalion, 35th Infantry, started upward, gained a lodgment on the crest and struck it there, taking terrible punishment and engaging throughout the night at hand-grenade range. The Third Battalion, 27th Infantry, closed in from the other end of the ridge to complete the kill. This action, the taking of Hill 440, was one of the most gallant episodes of the war in Korea.

But no Chinese retreat followed the fall of the hill. The

Millett's Men Marching Up

enemy still stood ready to contest every eminence and village beyond it. But with the linch-pin gone from the defense, the way was open for armor to strike along the main roads to the northward and, combining with infantry, destroy in detail the enemy forces clinging to the subordinate ridge-lines.

This was Operation Punch. Its unique feature was that it was a shuttle. The two task forces advanced a certain distance each day. The tanks, quad .50's, and supporting field artillery barraged a certain number of hills. The infantry, under this fire cover, swept the same ground clean. Then what was taken was given back, the task forces withdrawing to the main line of resistance (MLR) by early evening.

That night more Chinese came back into the ground. Next day the same show was repeated. It was a clean, killing performance, repeated with certain variations, for five days running. At the end, 4251 enemy bodies were counted on the ground. The American loss, including the fight for Hill 440, was less than seventy dead.

Millett's company was in the task force which advanced by the left-hand road that winds toward Inchon. What follows is a chapter in the success of Task Force Bartlett.

At noontime, on the first day out (5 February 1951), the First Platoon of Easy got pinned down in a frozen paddy while it was advancing against a low-lying ridge, from which the road column had received a scattering rifle fire. The Platoon then doused the hill crest liberally with fire from the 60-mm and 81-mm mortars. No real trouble was expected.

The line deployed and went forward. Quite suddenly, artillery, mortar and machine-gun fire ranged in on it, just as the lead files were approaching a draw that would have given them partial cover. The lead man, an ROK soldier, went down from a bullet. Behind him, Private First Class Johnnie Decrossett got two bullets through his legs, and a shell fragment winged him in the shoulder as he was falling. Lieutenant Don E. Wilson ran forward to drag the lead man back to cover but was stopped by a bullet before he could get to him. Sergeant First Class Floyd E. Cockrell, who had been moving with Wilson, ran out and dragged Wilson back to the cover of a ditch. He had been hit a second time. From over on the left of the paddy came the cry, "Two men are hit here!"

Then came temporary paralysis. Men moved only the distance required to get in under the paddy bank or near a hummock. Metal ripped into the ice all around them. Private First Class Eunis Bush, feeling an impulse to go forward, was checked by the sight of his mates lying flat and hardly even moving to return fire.

Millett, from his CP—a hole in the ground—fifty yards behind the rifles, had taken it all in. He called to the Second Platoon to come in on the First's left with bayonets fixed. Then he ordered his Third Platoon to support the attack with overhead fire from rifles, BAR's and the machine gun. The ground around him was already hot from artillery shell. Possibly he was happy enough to leave it as he ran

forward to the First Platoon, yelling, "Fix bayonets and follow me!" Two of the words of that order were superfluous.
The bayonets were already fixed, though flat down.

The men arose as he passed through them. From rearward, the Third Platoon's four BAR's and gun had opened
fire. From that ground, the men could see the hill from the
halfway mark and on up to the summit. The weapons kept
working perfectly.

Running straight to the base of the hill, Millett paused
there for about two minutes. Cockrell had come right on
behind him, but it took that long for the others to know
that they had to go—had to follow. There at the base, they
were briefly in defilade. The Second Platoon, coming in on
a different line, managed to join them without passing
through the zone of direct fire.

Glancing back, Millett assured himself that all had come
up save the wounded. Then he started up the slope, yelling,
"*She-lie sa-ni!*" which is supposed to be Chinese for "I'm
going to kill you with a bayonet," though I cannot vouch for
it.

Whether or no, it was the noise that carried them on, and
the noise that was important.

Others yelled, "Get out of your holes and fight, you bloody
bastards!"

Still others shouted, "Hubba-hubba! Hubba-hubba!" or
simply screamed in high pitch.

Once started, the chorus never slackened, though breath
grew short from the steepness of the climb. Private First Class
Carmen Nunno stumbled and fell into a ditch. The others
passed over him, and for the moment, quiet himself, his ear
was sensitive to the bedlam. The screaming, he said, made
his blood run cold. "I never thought you could get it out of
GI's."

Fortune, fickle as ever, picked a new favorite. Having been
bare to the fire on the low ground, the First Platoon, making
its climb, was protected by the bulging rock of the ridgeline.

The Chinese bullets whined harmlessly overhead. But the Second Platoon, which had won unscathed to its position on the left flank, became a shining target for menace from a new quarter. As the men climbed, their backs were turned to another ridge 150 yards away. This had been Fox Company's objective but Fox had not jumped off in time. The crest was alive with Chinese snipers, and their bullets found the range. A bend in the ridge masked the right flank to this fire, but the Second Platoon was getting it right in the back. Man after man went down. Millett was out ahead of the First Platoon like a hare leading on hounds. In the crisis of the moment, three men recognized that the Second Platoon had to solve its own local problem.

They were Sergeant Lee Buffington and Private First Class Edward Loder—a good hand with an M1—and Private First Class Gobel Marksbury, Jr., who toted a BAR. This was the trick. Loder worked about twenty-five yards to the right of the BAR, and on up the ridge about twenty feet higher than Marksbury, who, covered by Buffington's rifle, lay in partial concealment behind some scrub pine. Loder stood in the open and fired very rapidly a clip from his M1, aiming at the crest of the other ridge; then he dropped flat among the rocks. Immediately the enemy centered fire on him; Marksbury, with his BAR, and Buffington with his rifle picked off the men who were firing on Loder. It was good hunting, but the kind of game that can't last very long. They saw five or six enemy snipers crumple in their foxholes and others pick up and run over the skyline, while Loder played jack-in-the-box. Then a sniper's bullet found, not Loder, but Marksbury, getting him through the stomach. The round also destroyed his weapon. Buffington and Loder tried to continue the trick, using only their rifles. But the BAR had been the key to it, and there was no further good pay-off. However, it had worked long enough for salvation.

One litter team, formed from the clerical staff, moved with each platoon. Under fire, the hard-hit cases were evacuated from the hill as soon as they were down. But for the litter bearers, it was terrible going. The ice was thin on the canals and paddies. With their extra burden, they broke through and sank in mud and water up to their waists. Yet Marksbury was in a helicopter on his way to hospital within fifteen minutes of receiving his wound.

And like other infantrymen in Korea, Easy had thrown away its steel helmets. On this day the preponderant number of its wounded were hit in the neck or the head.

But no loss stayed the advance of the line. The men were on their way, their other leaders trying vainly to keep up with Millett as he strode up the slope, jumping over rock outcroppings with the ease of a gazelle, holding his rifle in his right hand, using his left to wave them on.

Cockrell, trying to keep pace with Millett, found it impossible. He continued a good second some ten or fifteen feet behind him, with Sergeant First Class Fred H. Hines hard on his heels, but also feeling himself outdistanced in the personal contest.

Back in the Third Platoon's position, machine gunner Corporal Robert L. Melzer and the BAR men and riflemen around him were sweating out the problem of how long they could hold their covering fire. They were giving the upper half of the hill everything their weapons had at a range of 250 yards. But the bayonet line had not yet come into view. They worried lest the men might be crawling upward, and missing the movement among the rocks, they would punish their own ranks.

It was a needless concern. Melzer, with his field glasses trained on the mid-slope, suddenly saw Millett standing clear and alone. He had faced about momentarily to urge the others on. Then Cockrell and Hines were framed in the glasses.

The Third Platoon's fire was now sweeping the crest. Raising his glasses to follow it, Melzer observed what Millett was not in position to see—that the tumult and momentum

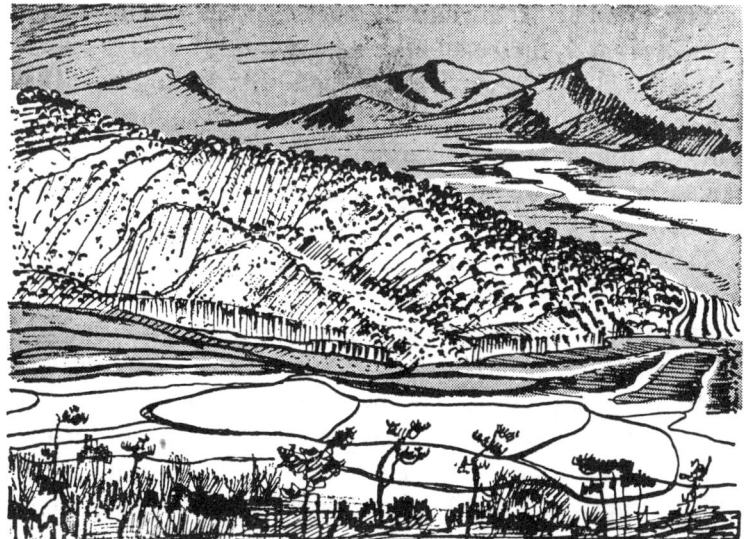

Millett's Hill 180

of the charge were already achieving their decisive effect. Along the skyline, the Chinese were quitting their bunkers and foxholes and disappearing over the far side of the slope.

Melzer had no chance to observe more. Private First Class Jackie Leffler, who had been shot through the head while making the climb with the Second Platoon, came staggering into the gun position. Melzer put down his glasses to attend to Leffler's wound.

The First Platoon got to the top without losing a man on the upgrade. But the willing bayonets were not given a chance. The enemy had departed in a rush, leaving a freshly served meal and numerous weapons behind in the well camouflaged positions. The Second Platoon, which had made the climb parallel to the Chinese line of withdrawal, shot a few of them down during the getaway. There was no pursuit. For the hour the Company settled down to a defense of the hill.

What had happened was by way of a full-dress rehearsal for the show staged two days later. In common with the greater number of "furious bayonet charges" reported from the Korean war, there had been no use of cold steel.

What had been shown mainly was that Millett and Easy together formed a combination ideally suited to shock action, and that a man standing upright to go in with the bayonet is a sucker for a bullet in the back of the head. Further experience was to develop no exception to these findings.

Task Force Bartlett continued its shuttle operation up and back along the left-hand road leading to the Han. By midmorning of 7 February, Easy Company was again heading into trouble. The Third Platoon was in a "reserve position" on its right rear, which meant simply that the Third was dug in on the top of a hill, prepared to fire forward, while the other two platoons advanced via the road ready to assault the next enemy-held ridge, with Millett leading them.

From the sharp vision and intuition of Private Victor Cozares came the pattern of the subsequent action. From the Third Platoon's hill he began to study the next ridge, 400 yards away. The armor and the rest of Easy were in the act of bypassing it. Cozares' eyes were drawn to the crest. It was dense with foliage. That was the trouble with it, he reflected—there was far *too much* growth at the top of an otherwise almost barren hill. Calling his discovery to the attention of others, he looked with field glasses. Finally, he saw the head of one man bob up and as quickly disappear. As his eyes steadied in the search, he saw more movement, and he could pick up foxholes behind the tree branches. By now, another half-dozen men were beside Cozares watching the hill; a small embankment screened them from the enemy. As they looked, a man arose from the enemy position and came walking straight toward them. Cozares said, "Hold fire!" But when the man had come halfway, a nervous soldier beside Cozares suddenly uncorked two shots. The man ran back over the ridge.

Lieutenant John T. Lammond called Millett on his SCR-536 and told him where the enemy force lay and that there were "many of them." Millett was 350 yards to his left, on the road, and abreast of the ridge. Millett told Lammond that the Third Platoon was to provide a covering fire from hill to hill with all weapons. The tanks were on the road slightly forward of Lammond's hill. They would move off the road, take position and fire on the same target.

Millett allowed himself just ten minutes to get his assault under way. His plan was to close with the First Platoon on the ridge at bayonet point under the Third's covering fire, while the Third held ready to come forward on the run if needed in the hand-to-hand fight. He radioed Lieutenant Raimund Schulz the word to get the First Platoon ready, and Schulz tried to relay it down the line.

This much done, Millett turned to the armor. Possibly he spent excessive time worrying about his supporting fires, and too little making sure that his men were set. He told the tankers to keep blasting the hill halfway up until he signalled a cease-fire. To make sure that the fire would be exact, he jumped on a tank, swung one of the .50's around, bull's-eyed it, fired a few rounds, and said, "Keep it there." Corporal Naiko and Private First Class Richard Dials were with him. They were given the signal and told to act for Millett if he became a casualty. All of this was talked out with the tank commander in three or four minutes. Then Millett and the two men started for the First Platoon.

Its position was no longer a placid one. Heavy return fire was now coming from the hill. Schulz and the greater part of his men were crouched down behind a large dike flanking the road. Between the dike and the ridge, seventy-five yards away, lay a deep ditch and a flat of frozen paddies. The dike was long enough to screen the rifle squad on the right and the machine-gun group in the center. But it left Buffington and the other rifle squad exposed to the cold breeze and the fire as well. Private James R. Turner tried to move forward a few yards to get behind a hummock. Just then Buffington got a call from Schulz to pull his squad in behind the dike.

He would have done so if the enemy machine gun hadn't already felled Turner. The bullet hit him in the ankle and turned down into the sole of his foot, immobilizing him. Buffington crawled out to drag and carry him to safety. Thus it happened that for a few important minutes, the twelve men on the left were leaderless and unprepared for the next move.

In the center, Sergeant Maynard Byers started replying with his machine gun at about the time when Schulz yelled to Buffington to contract to the right. Just as Turner was hit, the gun went dead from a ruptured cartridge. Byers bent to the task of freeing the gun. Several others joined him in his work, and still several others watched them. So in the center of the First Platoon's line also there was a little dead space, where there should have been concentration on the order.

Cockrell was on the extreme right when Millett came into the position running. As he came on, he yelled to Cockrell: "Get ready to move! We're going to assault the hill. Fix bayonets! Charge! Everybody goes with me!"

But he didn't stop. At a dog trot, he started across the ice-surfaced paddies, hurdling the banks which compartmented them, but keeping his feet as he came down on the next patch of ice. Other than a sad line of stunted Lombardy poplars, hung with magpies' nests—a common fixture of the Korean scene—nothing else intervened between him and the base of the hill. Bullets were chipping the ice all around as Cockrell and thirteen other men took out after him. They had moved in the nick of time. As they completed the run to the hill base, enemy rifles on the right joined the machine gun which had been firing from the left, and ice splinters filled the air forward of the dike. Several of Buffington's men, starting too late, were cut down as they ran across the ice.

In the Korean fighting the base of a hill was nearly always a friendly space. The enemy dug in around the knoll tops and in the saddles. So situated, he couldn't bring his flat-trajectory weapons to bear on men at the foot of the slope.

Reaching the bottom of Hill 180, Millett paused just long enough to catch his breath and give Schulz, Cockrell and the men time to catch up. For that moment, they were relatively safe. Feeling no pain because so few had made the crossing, Millett said to Cockrell, "It's pretty good, considering everything," and Cockrell grunted his agreement.

They had run toward the nose of Hill 180 at an angle. The lowest of three knobs marking 180's profile was immediately above their heads. Part of its rim was smoothed off and rounded in the conventional form of a Korean graveyard. The knob in the ridge's center and the last rise at the far end were some twenty meters higher. They expected to find the enemy strength disposed around the two higher elevations.

Millett started climbing on a straight line for the first knob. Getting almost to it, he stood on the skyline, waving for the others to come on, and yelling, "BAR! BAR!" From that ground, he could see the top position, 250 yards away. It was fairly crawling with enemy soldiers. He could also see the machine gun firing from the flank of the same position against his men on the low ground.

Private First Class Ray P. Velarde, who was carrying the BAR, was only a dozen strides behind Millett when he got the call. He had closed the distance by the time Millett topped the first rise. Seeing a foxhole next to the Captain's feet, he hopped into it. And seeing the live targets toward which Millett was pointing, he opened fire.

Millett strode on. Velarde saw him cock his arm back to throw a grenade. Not knowing whether he had found a live target at close range, Velarde still lowered his weapon, and swung it to the side to cover Millett.

Already the other thirteen had come up to them, scrambling over the ice-covered rocks, screaming like fiends, just as they had done two days before. Millett, his gaze still on the peak, hadn't really seen anything in the foreground. But the corner of his eye had caught a flash of motion, and from instinct he threw the grenade. As Velarde whirled Private Jim Chung, one of Easy's ROK soldiers, came abreast of Millett. He looked up at him, smiled, and said, "Captain, me shoot?" then pointed. Almost under Millett's feet were eight enemy soldiers, squatted in foxholes dug into the saddle not twenty feet away. Millett said, "Go ahead, Chung," and as the ROK emptied his M1 into them, Millett's rifle joined fire with him. He got two of them and Chung got some of the others. Then Millett threw two more grenades for good measure.

Velarde, taking it all in and realizing that his BAR wasn't needed at that point, aimed once again at the main enemy position and pulled the trigger. His first burst hit dead on the machine gun, wrecking the piece and killing the gunners.

Already the knob was buzzing with bullets and Millett's party could "feel the air stir with the volume of it." Velarde felt a swish next his cap, and a plucking at his shoulders. He was still whole-skinned but the enemy fire had neatly divested him of the tree camouflage he had worn on the upper part of his body.

Millett was still standing in the open, looking at the main position. What he saw was alarming. The high knob was honeycombed with diggings, circling the crest and running far down the slope. It was as active as an anthill. He saw several score of men moving in the open, but not a sign of preparation for withdrawal.

Cockrell, on the other hand, was worrying about the ground just ahead. He wasn't sure that Millett and Chung had cleaned it up. To his eye it seemed that there were other diggings beyond the holes which Millett had engaged. To test it, he threw a grenade; it went wild, rolled down the slope and exploded harmlessly. But from the ground at which he had aimed, three grenades came back. One landed next to Corporal George Swauger, exploded under his right leg, and shattered it. Lieutenant Schulz, who was beside Swauger, gave him first aid.

This incident, and what he had seen of the summit, put Millett to his decision. He called Lammond on his SCR-536, told him to ready the Third Platoon immediately and from his ridge charge frontally against 180. That would bring him in on Millett's right. During the few minutes while Lammond was forming his line on the crest, the group with Millett rested, if rest is the word for it.

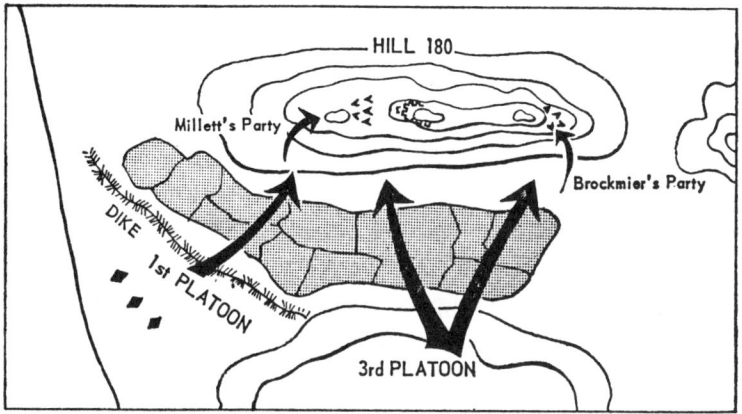

How Millett's Bayonet Charge Developed

No battle charge ever got off to a more spectacular or less promising start. Until the Third Platoon started down their hill at a dead run, none had realized that the down slope was all the way a glare of ice. Millett, watching Lammond's line from 180, saw it top the rise and then disintegrate, as man after man lost his footing, landed on his rump and coasted down the hill like a toboggan. Miraculously, most of them managed to hold on to their weapons. From the enemy ground, burp guns over on the right, a machine gun halfway up the hill in the center, and the nests of riflemen deployed around the two upper knobs turned their undivided fire against this sliding, careening mass.

The slide down the slope was about fifty yards. The run from hill to hill was another 150 yards on the flat. Regaining its feet, the Third Platoon took off at a bound across this expanse of ice-bound paddies. Not one man lagged behind. They charged, screaming and cursing, dead ahead, seemingly unheeding the rain of bullet and shell which was cracking the ice under their feet.

Some of the fire found its mark. Private First Class Howard Baumgardner was knocked down by two bullets. One slug had cut his BAR sling and the other had knocked out the rear sight. He was unhurt, though a trifle rump-sprung. Picking himself up, he rejoined the charge, though he was now weaponless. Then a piece of mortar shell hit him in the leg and a bullet tore away the seat of his trousers. He went down again, picked himself up again, and kept on running toward the hill.

Private First Class John W. Lescallet, carrying the Platoon's machine gun, miraculously made the run downhill without falling. Crossing the paddies, he was knocked down by a mortar hit that ruined the bipod. But he kept on with the weapon. Then a bullet hit the gun over the latch cover and ruined it. Throwing the gun away, Lescallet kept on going. He still had his pistol. Within five minutes, the Third Platoon had closed against the base of 180. Though its ranks were bruised, skinned-up and bullet-nicked, all were still alive and fighting.

In his few minutes of organizing the charge, Lammond had done a neat bit of figuring. He placed himself on the extreme left so that he would arrive at Hill 180 on a line even with Millett. Then he extended the Platoon line far to the rightward. By increasing the interval between men, he would give the enemy less of a target and would also approach the hill in formation to attack it along its entire length.

These dispositions worked out as foreseen. Millett walked down to meet him as the Platoon completed its run. He

said briefly, "Attack straight up the hill!" Lammond turned
to shout that order to Sergeant First Class Donald Brockmier,
who was leading the group on the Third Platoon's extreme
right flank. But Brockmier had already gone. Along with
Lescallet, Corporal Marshall E. Fletcher, Corporal Joseph E.
Cyr and Sergeant Robert E. Blair, he had deployed to the
extreme end of the hill. This handful was already toiling up
the slope intent on closing around the enemy's rear.

They started hopefully enough. There were two BAR's
in the party. The others except Lescallet had grenades and
M1's. Bounding about five yards at a time, the grenadiers
worked over the foreground while the automatic rifles supplied a covering fire. The system was perfect while it
worked; the will of the group was limitless, but its strength in
men and supply was not equal to the task. So in the end it
suffered the hardest fortune of the day.

Already, however, hell was popping elsewhere. Millett's
brief instruction to Lammond ended in a detonation as two
grenades came sailing down on them from the same saddle
Chung had engaged in the opening minutes. Millett turned
and ran straight up to the enemy works. Right on his heels
was Corporal Herbert Faulkner, who had arrived with Lammond. On reaching the crest, he was about ten yards to
Millett's left, which put him within fifteen feet of the enemy
foxholes, though he had not previously known their location.
Too late, he saw his mistake, but he couldn't retreat. An
enemy "buffalo gun" (antitank rifle) was pointing right at
his head twelve feet away. He ducked to one side as the gun
went off, then dodged to the other as it roared again.

For five rounds this mad dance continued. Then a grenade
came at him. In jumping away from its blast, he fell behind a rock, but it was too flat even to shield his head. He lay
there for a moment thinking it was the end. Then the fire
lifted. From behind the rock he yelled to Millett as loud as he
could: "Get them if you can! I can't. They're sniping right
at me."

But Millett didn't hear a word. He didn't even know
Faulkner was there. His ear was dulled to the noise of the
explosions right next him by the general noise of the battle.
Still puzzled as to the exact location of the enemy foxholes,
he stood there in the open, looking in the wrong direction.
A moment too late he turned, saw the buffalo gun firing in
the opposite direction, and realized his danger. The enemy
had reacted not less slowly to his presence, though right then,
to Faulkner's good fortune, the target shifted to Millett.
Eight grenades came at Millett, five of which exploded, as
he ducked and twisted like an African dodger. From twenty
yards down the slope, Sergeant Hines was witnessing this
scene.

He yelled, "Look out!" The ninth grenade had landed
right behind Millett and he hadn't seen it. Its explosion drove
a piece of steel into Millett's back. Apart from a considerable
blood-letting, which was possibly helpful, its main effect was
to make Millett realize that if he persisted on this line, it
would be suicide.

Instead of walking straight into the foxholes along the line
of the ridge, he now determined to work over to the reverse
crest and come in on the left flank of the enemy position. So
he set out to circle the lower knob, a movement which took
him through the ground held by Schulz and his group and
brought him out slightly above the left flank of the Third
Platoon's line. These men had been concentrating their fire
from the lower knob against the high hilltop. The guns of
the armor should have been firing on the same target. But
in his preparation, Millett had directed them to fire along a
line halfway up the hill, where they were doing little or no
damage, and he didn't think to change the order. Much too
late, he regretted that mistake.

In making his detour, Millett passed Cockrell, who asked
him: "Shall we try to take prisoners?" Millett answered: "I
say to hell with it. No one on this hill intends to give up."

As he rounded the ridge and came out just above the Third

Platoon's flank, its ranks heard him shouting: "Use grenades and cold steel! Use grenades and cold steel! Come on up here, you sons of bitches!"

The language surprised them. They had never heard the Captain talk like that. They were shocked, but not made unhappy. They commented to one another on how they could hear and see Millett above all else on the field. The red mustache now bristled straight out. The fighting face was flushed almost scarlet. And with all hands yelling *"she-lie"* and words unprintable, Millett's piercing voice could still be heard above all others.

The Third Platoon was doing its work boldly but methodically, and it would not be rushed. On the left flank, nearest Millett, Cozares was leading an attack group which included Privates First Class Bush and Harold E. Blodgett. Cozares, acting as point, spent his own two grenades on an enemy foxhole about halfway up the ridge. Then he yelled for the others to pitch him grenades baseball-style. Bush had one and Blodgett two; the four men spread out on either side of them had a total of six. In the same way that an infield tosses the ball around prior to an inning, they kept Cozares supplied through the air. The advance proceeded by bounds, ten to twelve feet a time. Cozares, catching the grenade, unpinned and threw it, and as he yelled, "Grenade!" all went flat. Then another grenade was pitched to him, and the whole group bounded forward to the edge of the area just struck, there repeating the process. In this way they bombed out a path for themselves right to the skyline; in so doing they had killed perhaps a dozen of the enemy. Cozares had an unerring aim.

Over on the far end of the hill, Brockmier and his group of four, having proceeded in about the same way as Cozares, were now almost atop the ridge, but were about to run out of grenades and BAR ammunition. The BAR's had raked the cap of Hill 180. The firers had seen a number of men fall. Things were getting much quieter up there. Cyr, Blair,

Lescallet and Fletcher were still going along strongly. But what worried Brockmier was another hill, 250 yards to his rear. Bullets were chipping the rocks around his party and he sensed from the whine of the ricochets that they couldn't be coming from the ground he was engaging.

This was how the fight stood about forty minutes after it had started. Easy had moved about as fast as is humanly possible under combat condtions. All around the perimeter developments were approaching their tremendous climax. Bayonets were still pointed forward: they had not been used.

Back on the skyline again, Millett came out within five feet of the enemy diggings from which he had been grenaded. He walked toward the hole firing his M1. So well was it covered with tree branches and piled-up earth that he could get no idea what the trench held.

But in the midst of fire, at the far end, he saw the buffalo gun swing around. He went straight in with the bayonet. His blade sank into a Chinese throat and tore through the neck. He had to fire the M1 to release its bayonet by the recoil. In the nick of time he was able to get the blade into the throat of a second man coming at him with a clubbed rifle.

That, he thought, cleaned up the situation. But Private Nunno, standing at the trench a few feet from Millett, saw a third man stoop low to crawl through a passage back to the buffalo gun. Nunno tried to fire, but there was just an empty click from his rifle. So he jumped into the trench. Three times he lunged, trying to bayonet the man. Each time the blade slipped off his thick clothing. On the fourth thrust it sank between the shoulder blades and the man died.

Cockrell had rushed forward to Millett's support. Even as Nunno jumped into the trench, Cockrell saw another head rise up out of the ground ten yards behind Millett in a hitherto concealed hole. He jumped toward it, and his bayonet went downward into the man's neck and chest cavity. Hot blood spurted into his face. A second figure arose from behind the corpse, but there was no motion of surrender. Cockrell shot him square between the eyes at one-foot range.

Cockrell's move had flushed yet a third group. Nunno saw a man's head bob up from a camouflaged pit just a few yards on beyond the Sergeant. He charged the spot even as Cozares' party, coming at last to the skyline, converged on the same ground at a right angle to his run. Nunno was going fast, holding the bayonet straight out, with his full body weight behind it. The blade tore straight through the man's chest and stuck there, the victim dying almost instantly. From the same foxhole tier, two more men arose, rifles in hand. Blodgett, running to Nunno's assistance, blew their heads off with his BAR.

Cozares and Bush had topped the rise some twenty yards beyond Blodgett. They screamed like Apaches as they turned right along the ridgeline to continue the mop-up. Immediately, Cozares spied two Chinese crouching low in a foxhole, not ten feet away. Both held rifles pointed on the Americans. Cozares pulled his trigger; one man slumped over, shot through the head. He pulled again, and the rifle clicked dead; the M1 ejector had failed at that moment; the second cartridge had not gone into the chamber.

That gave the second Chinese time to fire; Cozares, lunging toward him, felt the bullet singe his ear at seven-foot distance. At the last split second the man turned, and Cozares' bayonet went through his back. As he withdrew the blade, a third enemy soldier jumped from a foxhole on the reverse slope and ran past him; Cozares sprinted after him and the chase ended as his blade spitted the man between the shoulders. He cleared his rifle and got another shell into the chamber just in time to shoot a fourth man who had jumped from a trench a few yards on ahead, and started to run. Cozares sprang for the trench; it was split in two by a bank of earth. At first he saw only the empty ditch; then the fifth man stood up clear just beyond the embankment. Cozares' knees hit the earth bank at the same instant his bayonet went through the man's chest. The sensation almost overpowered him, for to his shock and amazement, the chest, on being pierced, gave forth a booming sound "like a bass drum." By now his every motion was mechanical and he was screaming uncontrollably. Something stirred in the covered portion of the trench beyond the man who had just fallen; a sixth man was crawling down the passage, trying to get away. Cozares killed him with another shot from the M1, not even bothering to put his rifle to his shoulder.

And momentarily, he must have gone a little mad. Uncertain that the fifth man was dead, he turned back to give him more. Four times he drove the bayonet into the chest, and each time he heard the same dreadful boom. It heightened his hysteria. On the fourth withdrawal, he drove straight at the man's head. The blade wedged in the skull. For five minutes he strained to loosen it, sweating and screaming.

That struggle, and one thing else, brought him back to sanity. While he tugged at the blade, Private First Class Takashi Shoda passed him and continued on along the ridge. Shoda was a BAR man. He marched straight ahead, shifting his weapon from left to right and blasting every shrub or bit of ground that looked as if it might conceal an enemy. He acted like a man with a mission, paying no heed to anyone else. But as he moved he laughed a terrible laugh which rose above every other sound on the field. It kept on and on like something out of a bad dream or a lunatic ward. After Shoda had passed from sight, Cozares could still hear it. The sound frightened him; it also made him feel better. He wasn't the only one.

Faulkner, the man who had dodged the buffalo gun, moved down the ridge, the same way as Shoda. He passed the halfway point uneventfully; Shoda had mopped up well. Then just a few strides from him an enemy soldier popped out of a hole, rifle in hand. Faulkner charged; the bayonet went through the man's neck but didn't kill him. The man lay there for perhaps ten minutes, though to Faulkner it seemed an hour. While the blood spurted from the wound, he tried to speak but couldn't. He made feeble gestures with his hands. Faulkner guessed that he was begging to be killed. But Faulkner made no move. He couldn't kill the man; he couldn't pull away. He just sat there watching until the man died.

At the far end of the ridge Brockmier and his group had gotten almost to the cap of Hill 180. With the mop-up completed there, the whole ridge would be in Easy's hands, though Brockmier had no way of knowing how the rest of the Company was faring. The BAR clips were empty now but their fire had almost pacified the high ground.

It looked at that moment as if the goal were in sight; but as events transpired for this group the distance was infinite.

In front of them, two Chinese arose from a foxhole.

Brockmier threw a grenade—his last one. It hit fair but did the work only partially.

Blair rushed the hole with his bayonet to finish it.

Lescallet, standing beside Brockmier, spun and fell. A bullet had gotten him right through the back of the head.

So died the hard-going private soldier who had kept on charging with his pistol after his machine gun had been shot from his hands.

Brockmier didn't even have time to stop and feel for heart action. He heard a cry from Blair, who was still standing by the foxhole. Then Blair toppled and rolled a few yards down the slope. He had been killed just as was Lescallet, with a bullet through the back of his head.

The other three left the bodies there near the two enemy dead and moved on up toward the skyline.

Above them, a few yards on, a man arose from a foxhole, his arm looping back to toss a grenade. Fletcher charged him with his bayonet, ran it through his chest and killed him.

As he withdrew the blade, a bullet coming from rearward hit Fletcher in the back of the head and he fell dead.

With Brockmier now there was only Cyr. It came to Brockmier's mind that he had better give it up, return to the base of the hill and work back toward the Platoon, or else they would all be killed.

He said to Cyr, "I think we've had enough," and the other man nodded.

There was a stirring under some dead tree branches hard by them. Cyr rushed toward the spot with his bayonet forward. An enemy soldier tried to arise from the camouflaged foxhole. Cyr pinned the man there, killing him.

Then, as Cyr straightened, a bullet hit him in the back of the head and he died instantly.

After that, Brockmier didn't care. With Cyr's death he forgot about rejoining the Platoon. He felt it was too late—that all luck had run out. He continued moving and fighting on the same line he had been taking.

Two more Chinese arose in his path. Their backs were turned to him; they seemed to be looking at something coming from the other direction. He shot them before they knew he was there.

That cost him his last bullet.

Twenty yards or so farther along, another man arose, standing with his back toward Brockmier. Moving along stealthily for a distance, Brockmier bounded the last few yards. In the final instant the man turned. It was not a strong thrust, because Brockmier was almost spent. But by accident it hit just the right spot in the neck and the man died without a struggle.

Brockmier walked on along the skyline, his rifle empty, his arms almost too tired to hold it. That was how he met Easy's skirmishers coming from the other direction.

The worst agony of the fight had closed around this one man. Every American killed on Hill 180 had died next to Brockmier.

There is little else to the story of Hill 180, as to how men hoped, planned and feared, how they fought, where they died and what blows they dealt the enemy.

Easy Company's use of cold steel was not marked by any parade-ground finesse. All hands had learned something on that point. Millett had watched his men during the worst of the in-fighting. He told them later, chiding just a bit, that not a one of them had used the strokes he had taught. When life was at stake, they had cut and slashed every which way. It remained for Cozares to tell him in front of the others, "I watched you, too, Captain, and you didn't make one stroke correctly, according to your own teaching."

The noise and fury did not all end with the dispatch of the last enemy. The enemy had staked out some animals on the hill—two Mongolian ponies and a jackass. With blood still up, some of Easy's men went on to slaughter these dumb creatures. That was senseless, but so is war.

Shoda's hysterical laughter still sounded over the field.

The others had ceased their yelling and screaming. But they danced around, pounding one another on the back and saying: "We're good! We're good! We're good!"

To this estimate which they made of themselves, even history would say they were entitled. It had not been a perfect show: there is none such where men fight. But together they had staged the most complete bayonet charge by American troops since Cold Harbor.

That evening, as they organized for perimeter defense of Hill 180, they had time to make careful check of what had been done. The armored people were very admiring and greatly obliging. They agreed to outpost the hill on the roadward side.

Of the approximately two hundred men in the mixed force of Chinese and North Koreans which had been holding Hill 180, forty-seven lay dead on the ground. Of these eighteen had been killed with the bayonet. The wounds proved it beyond question.

Among the booty captured were three buffalo guns, two heavy machine guns, one light machine gun, one tommy gun, thirty-seven rifles.

About two miles north of Hill 180 lies a nameless Korean village. There the enemy had set up a first-aid station. When on the next day the village passed into our hands, the natives said that sixty enemy wounded had been evacuated from Hill 180 during the fight to be treated among them. These and other survivors had slipped away by the back door, which Brockmier and his group were too few to cover wholly.

Unless the weather has knocked it down, or some fell hand removed it, there is a bayonet stuck into the crack of a rock atop Hill 180 holding a sign which reads: "Compliments of Easy Company."

Other tokens of the day will outlast that one.

Captain Millett, who aspired to be a worthy successor to a courageous leader named Desiderio, also got the Medal of Honor and lived to tell it.

Easy Company won another Distinguished Unit Citation.

On this one the awards boards didn't dare split fine hairs about what constitutes high action "above and beyond the call."

LAST BARRIER

Hearing It from the Marines

WHEN I returned from Korea in the late spring of 1951, it was my intention to write a book about the fight of the 1st Marine Division in the far north which would be a companion to the story about the defeat of the 8th Army, *The River and the Gauntlet*. I even had a similar title for it; it was to be called *The Canyon and the Lake*. My field notes on that operation were as complete as for the journal about the 8th Army fight north of Kunuri, and many of the marine commanders had entrusted to me some of their basic documents such as the overlays used on their long patrols. But immediately I became sidetracked in writing two book-length operation analyses of our tactics and weapons effects in the police action for official purposes, and by the end of it I was fed to the teeth on writing about Korea. There is, however, in the locked files a detailed analysis of Marine operations in November, December 1950, which I did at the time so that other U.N. forces might profit from the lessons.

The circumstances which created the opportunity for this work were unique; I would guess that there have been few times in history when an army officer has served in any such role with the United States Marines in the field. But then, the situation in which American forces found themselves after the Chinese Communists entered the war with a vengeance were also a bit unusual. From the time of my arrival in Korea I had argued with everyone who would listen to me, and especially with my associates in G-3 at 8th

Army, that our use of company-size perimeters in night defense was tactically unsound and deplorable. I put it about this way: "This front is so far overstretched that we are going to be penetrated anyway. There is no way to prevent it when our line is so thin. The question is what to do about it. When you use company perimeters and the unit is hit and becomes threatened with envelopment, in any hard-pressed fight the supply of ammunition present cannot last more than five or six hours. Then the unit must withdraw. But if a battalion is engaged under the same circumstances, and is together in one perimeter, even though it is experiencing four or five times the pressure of the company, it should be able to hold out from three to four days. That is so because of the nature of troops. The larger the force present, the stronger becomes the morale of the general body and the less the tendency to panic fire or to paralysis among the firers. Additionally a battalion can usually maintain an effective reserve whereas a company cannot."

Especially after my experience with the 2d Infantry Division, following the withdrawal from Kunuri, I renewed the argument. A large part in the making of the disaster which overtook the 2d was that is used company perimeters all along the line and none had been able to hold out for more than a few hours, though the troops had fought to the limit. At the time when I returned to Seoul to report to the staff of 8th Army my conclusions about the fight of the 2d Division and the nature of the new enemy, the Marines were still heavily embattled in the far north and the 5th and 7th Regiments were about to begin their withdrawal from Udam-ni.

I said to my friend, Colonel John Dabney (later Lieutenant General), then the G-3 of 8th Army: "I am convinced the Marines must be using battalion perimeter at a minimum; if they were not, they would already have been more than half destroyed, with little chance of getting out."

John replied: "Why don't you fly over and see?"

That any such trip was necessary speaks volumes concerning the mismanagement of that phase of the war. The army and the independent corps were supposed to be joined in a common endeavor. But not only was there a gap of many miles between their flanks so that they had no feel of one another; overhead communications between them were virtually nonexistent. Because of this lack of information we were making errors on our front which might have been avoided had we received the lessons from their experience, and we could have saved them terrible hardship had they known some of the things that earlier happened to us. This is a helluva way to run a railroad!

When my mission became outlined, there was a great trembling in the camp. It was feared that I might be regarded as a spy. So some very weighty letters were prepared for me at Army and Corps Headquarters, by way of introduction, so that I would not be given the bum's rush. I threw them in the wastebasket before my departure, which is a recommended procedure in the handling of such nonsense.

I went first to Colonel Alpha Bowser (later Major General), who was G-3 of 1st Marine Division. He took me immediately to General Smith, whose words I put down as he said them because they were promptly entered in my notes. Smith said: "Colonel Marshall, we heard you were coming. We know about your work in the past. I have already called up my regimental commanders and told them that all personnel are to give you absolute cooperation. This division has nothing to hide. If you have any trouble anywhere along the line, come back and tell me; but I don't believe you will have any difficulty."

And he was right all the way!

The story about Schmuck's battalion, though only one of many that I collected, alone was shaped into a completed narrative. The irony of it is that in this fight the battalion used company perimeters. The only other outstanding instance in which this was done by troops of the division was the defense by Fox Company, 7th Regiment between Hagaru-ri and Udam-ni. In both cases the circumstances prohibited any alternative. Now and then war pays off with a few solid personal satisfactions. During my dealings with the two companies who fought on the highest and iciest hill scaled by any troops during the Korean war the two commanders spoke. I quote the words of one: "We both read *Men Against Fire,* in fact we almost memorized it. We trained our men according to its ideas and they paid off big. Our men went in yelling; they could see terror in the faces of the enemy. Our NCO's kept checking along the fire line. These things helped see us through."

Last Barrier I

ONLY a few years have passed since the Chosin Reservoir operation, but enough time to warrant saying that history already is selling it short. By the people it is remembered mainly as a fight marked by endurance and inspiration in heroic dimension. That is good so far as it goes, but it is not enough by half.

No other operation in the American book of war quite compares with this show by the 1st Marine Division in the perfection of tactical concepts precisely executed, in accuracy of estimate of situation by leadership at all levels, and in promptness of utilization of all supporting forces.

From these things, which are the epitome of power conservation, came in natural flow the extraordinary spirit which supercharged the fighting. And this, I truly believe, is the main point—that the battle from Chinhung-ni to Yudam-ni needs to be studied and remembered as a classic example in the application of means. For it is ever the way with fighting men that they will do their utmost when they know beyond doubting that the utmost is being done for them by those who lead.

The lesson of the Reservoir is that inspiration in war develops out of a solid base of realism. Of the operation came a phrase now justly celebrated: "We are not retreating; we are attacking in a new direction."

Shortly after the event, an Army friend said to me: "That was beautiful but it was bunk; it was not an appeal to reason."

What my friend mistook, not having studied the operation, was that the saying rang out over the battle because it was a considered reckoning of the tactical fact. At the hour in which it was uttered, the main weight of the enemy was pressing on the division flanks and rear. The main battle having gone awry elsewhere, no decisive object remained except the killing of the maximum number of Chinese. It was as simple as that.

But there was one battalion whose portion it became to attack in the old direction—due north. First Battalion of 1st Marines had come but recently to Chinhung-ni, and there composed the hedgehog farthest south covering the road to the base port. Between Chinhung-ni and Koto-ri, on which the main body of the division was moving, there was interposed a mountain height of almost Alpine character, solidly bunkered and garrisoned by the enemy. It became the mission of Lieutenant Colonel Donald M. Schmuck's men to destroy this bastion so that the passage of the division might be eased through the most dangerous defile in North Korea.

This study deals exclusively with the operations of the First Battalion, 1st Marines. By the circumstances in which the division initially was deployed, the battalion was engaged more briefly than any other fighting element. If its fighting accomplishment is worthy of remark, it therefore must still be noted that this unit experienced less than the others in unremitting strain.

On 29 November 1950, the American main supply route was cut by the enemy between Chinhung-ni and Koto-ri. The closure was but one minor part of an enemy buildup and onfall which, organized in the preceding days against all portions of the division column, then holding the main villages along fifty-eight miles of road, closed violently against the whole Marine deployment within a twenty-four-hour period. For the manner in which this envelopment was staged, the enemy is entitled to his share of credit. He had a plan promising total entrapment, and he held to it undeviatingly, though his difficulties of weather, communications, and transport were enormous. That in the end his resources were proved inadequate does not minimize the fact that in the beginning his aim and timing were well-nigh perfect.

The First Battalion at Chinhung-ni was hit from the west in the same hour that the road was cut between the Battalion and the division. It was a probe, delivered in such way as to leave the Battalion commander doubtful whether the object was harassment or a feeling-out preparatory to assault in strength. But he decided at once that the best policy was counterattack. A number of North Korean civilians had entered his perimeter. They told him that the Chinese, in the number of "several companies," had dug in along the ridges 1200 yards to the westward and were jam-packed in the villages on the low ground. They had seen the positions; they described in detail the locations; the truth of this information was confirmed by subsequent operations.

The valley winding westward from Chinhung-ni is a mere slit between the ubiquitous ridges. There was scarcely room at any point for a rifle platoon to deploy in line across its floor. The First Battalion hit westward on the morning of 30 November, taking two rifle companies and one battery of artillery, and moving in column.

But along the ridgetops to both sides of the column there advanced patrols in platoon strength. With the patrols went mortarmen and forward observers. About 1000 yards west of Chinhung-ni, the column drew its first fire from a platoon of enemy dug in along the lower ridge folds above a point where the valley narrowed almost to a dead end. By then the patrols already had the enemy position outflanked; they closed in and destroyed the blocking party with no loss to the column.

This small success was the pattern in embryo for all that followed. Four fighter aircraft had been ordered up for the attack on the main enemy positions. The defensive array was cut to order for the offensive arrangements which Schmuck had already made. Approximately one squadron of Chinese cavalry had come into the valley. Subsequently, the mounts had been withdrawn westward, but the discovery of several large, well-fertilized tethering spots showed that the force had come riding. It was disposed around two villages on the valley floor. Part of the force, probably the headquarters element, held to the houses. The deployed element was foxholed-in along the ridges on both sides of the settlement over a length of 400–600 yards. But these were not skyline positions. They were so placed along the slopes that their fire would bear upon the road coming from the eastward. The First Battalion's patrols on the ridgetops were therefore already pinching toward the enemy works when the column in the valley drew first fire.

Thereafter, the elimination of these positions was an exercise by the clock. The force was already out of radio contact with its base, but wire had been strung back to the battalion operations center. The flank patrols had a good view of the most forward enemy positions, and their forward observers took over. The attack opened with ten minutes of fire by the 4.2 mortars, followed by a shelling from the howitzers. Then waiting a minute or so for the smoke to clear so that the target could be cleanly defined, the 4.2's marked the spot with white phosphorus smoke under the direction of the mortarmen with the patrols. The four planes were already on station. Under control by the forward observers with the flank patrols, they struck with rockets and napalm. As the air attack ended, more 4.2 fire was put on the ridges, holding till the last moment while the rifle parties from the valley made the closing rush.

This was the formula applied throughout, with minor exceptions, in the cross-buck by which the Chinese holdings west of Chinhung-ni were fragmented. Part of the time the tactical air control party traveling with the road column had the Chinese Communist works under direct observation and therefore controlled the planes. They directed the strike against the villages, and despite the constriction of the valley, they saw the planes get in low enough to blow Chinese gunners from machine-gun pits dug in next to the houses.

It was a rout. The hill positions were rended knob by knob. At the end, the Chinese who survived along the low ground tried to take it on the lam, making for a valley exit wending to the northward. The hour being about 1600, Schmuck held his infantry in place for a return to base. But the air continued a strafing chase for as long as there were Chinese to see.

One detail remained; Marines put the torch to everything in sight which might provide shelter to a man. The villages were ablaze when the Battalion marched back.

So described in outline, the fight reads like a field day for heavy weapons, with just a little guidance from the foot force. As to shock effect, it was that. But it was estimated that of the Chinese killed on this ground (they numbered several hundred) eighty per cent were dispatched by small arms fire delivered at less than 200 yards range. The enemy had defended with mortars, machine guns, and rifles but had been unable at any point to get a killing fire going. There had been no use of the grenade.

Chinhung-ni was not again threatened from the west following this foray. Its next few days were quiet. The enemy moved south looking for a softer touch. He seemed to find it at Sudong-ni, two miles down the road, where a Marine engineer platoon, under Lieutenant Glendinning, was holding forth next to a power plant. On 6 December the Chinese invested the engineer unit, their automatic fire from the ridge above the village searing its camp and effectively blocking the road to the north. The platoon commander flew an American flag from his command post. An early volley cut it down. He personally put it up again and told his men that it would be kept there. Then he sent word to the First Battalion, 1st Marines that he would probably need help if he was to extricate his force. One reinforced platoon with a quad-50 and an artillery forward observer were sent south. The quad and the battery at Chinhung-ni brought the enemy-held ridge under fire. When the moment for withdrawal arrived, the flag was lowered, and the platoon marched out, covering the trucks in which its wounded were riding. Last out of the position was a bulldozer—blade-high— "The damnedest sight," said Schmuck, "that I ever saw."

All along, Schmuck had felt certain that someone would have to attack north when the division wheeled south, and he reckoned that the finger pointed toward him. One of his first actions had been to ask U.S. X Corps G-2 at Ham-hung for aerial photos of the country to the northward—an almost unheard-of asset in Korean operations. Three days later he got the photos. That had happened on 1 December, five days before the call came through from the engineer platoon which signaled that the Chinese were across its rear. Looking the obliques over and noticing the harsh aspect of the ridges, the Battalion commander decided that he had better scout the defile to the north well in advance of any order to attack in that direction, even though the enemy held it in strength.

On 2 December he sent a patrol northward along the canyon. Its mission, "to determine how far it could advance toward Koto-ri." The patrol was kept small in hope that it could make a sneak run. But it was heavy with authority. Attached to the rifle squad which went forward under Lieutenant Cooper were an artillery forward observer, Major Bates, the Weapons Company commander, and finally the commanding officer of the Battalion.

As a decoy to cover the movement of the reconnaissance patrol, a rifle platoon was sent north along the canyon one hour before Cooper got underway. It was told to move via the railroad tracks, remain in the open, make no particular effort at concealment, and retire if engaged.

The Battalion commander's group moved via the canyon road for the first leg of the distance, barreling along rapidly in three jeeps and one 2½-ton. The passage was uninterrupted. At the last bend in the road just prior to reaching the great powerhouse which figures prominently in the division story, the convoy stopped. The vehicles were turned about so that they faced down-canyon. The drivers were left there to guard them; Schmuck led the patrol forward afoot, its members hugging the embankment.

They passed the power plant and approached the first bend beyond it, still having seen no sign of life. But as they made the turn and scanned the ridges north and to the left of the road, the vista was like that described in the Song of Roland: "The valley and the mountains are covered with them; great are the hosts of this strange people." For as far as the eye could carry, the ridgetops ascending to Koto-ri were alive with enemy soldiers in such number that the men deemed it useless to attempt to count them.

The first startled reaction was a sunk feeling that the Chinese must have the patrol under observation. Then it was concluded this could not be so; the whole bearing of the people opposite, as studied through glasses, was casual and normal. They were behaving much as Americans might do, some laughing and talking together, some shaking out blankets, others digging or hacking away at brushwood.

The patrol moved north one more turn, then slipped up through a draw to left of the road and came out on a ridgetop within perhaps 300 yards of the nearest visible enemy position. From there it could see almost to Koto-ri.

Schmuck and Major Bates had remained on the road with the radio. The moment came when Schmuck felt he could resist temptation no longer. His whole foreground was an array of artillery targets. He would never get the same chance again. It was just a matter of calling for the fires and bringing them in as quickly and in as great volume as possible.

The artillery forward observer was with the group which had climbed to the ridgetop. He could raise the guns in Koto-ri. After he was briefed on the fire mission, it was agreed that control would be passed back and forth between the canyon road and the peak, according to which targets looked the best at the moment.

As the first salvo hit dead on, the Chinese were still standing bunched on the skyline. They broke for cover, moving in all directions, but they did not go fast enough. There followed a few minutes of slaughter grim and great. Said Colonel Schmuck of that experience: "It was the most rewarding few minutes of my whole period of service."

But it could not hold long. The patrol was told to fall back on the run. Everyone legged it down the canyon and the vehicles were underway by the moment the last man had loaded. It was a close thing. As the convoy took the dip where the road ran under the railway track, it missed interception by 150 yards or less by a Chinese party in company strength marching south along the right-of-way. On radio the decoy platoon was told to fall back on Chinhung-ni immediately. Both groups rejoined without having received one round of hostile fire.

A more decisive patrol action than this one can scarce be imagined. It gave the Battalion priceless knowledge of how the country looked and where it could expect to meet the enemy.

The personal effect on the leader was no less pronounced: "From that hour, I felt that I was in good position to attack up the canyon and I was confident we could carry it."

The attack westward had served to give the battalion a free hand in its own neighborhood and it used the respite in preparing to the fullest for further offensive action.

As to the effect on higher levels of this aggressive action, it can be measured by the words of the man in command. On 7 December, the 1st Marine Division reached Koto-ri. Of how the Division stood in that hour, Major General Oliver P. Smith said: "Knowing that Schmuck was there and that his men had already given a working-over to the ridges commanding the road running down the mountainside did more than all else to convince the division that the operation would be successfully completed. I sensed that feeling at Koto-ri. The very air had a lift to it. The column was dog-tired but all forebodings of failure had suddenly disappeared. That night I heard singing in the tent next to mine. It came from our drivers. They were singing the Marine Hymn, and doing it in a spirit of exultation. It was quite a remarkable thing. We were aware that great difficulties still confronted us, that the blown-out bridge had to be repaired and that the road ahead ran through an ice-covered mountain pass. But we discounted the dangers because we knew that Schmuck had already been over the ground."

On the same day the First Battalion, 1st Marines got order to attack north at 0800 on the following morning. The order remained subject to confirmation by regiment in the hour when it became certain that the division would attack from the north coincidentally. That day at 2310 the Battalion was relieved in place by Third Battalion, 7th Infantry Regiment (TF Dog) which had cut through the resistance in the lower valley, and Schmuck proceeded immediately to move his troops to an assembly area north of Chinhung-ni.

The Battalion was pointed toward the same commanding ridge where the patrol had completed its reconnaissance. Its first objective was the southwestern nose of the ridgeline embracing Hill 1081. Objective 2 was the hill itself, and the sub-ridges extending northward from it, the mass of which dominated the hairpin turn in the main supply route (MSR). These were the loftiest crags against which any American attack was launched during the war in Korea. Once in the Battalion's hands, they were to be held until the division had passed down the mountainside. The Battalion would then fall in as rear-guard.

This was the plan: to move out in column of companies under the cover of dark, take Objective 1 with the lead company as soon after first light as possible, and pass the two remaining companies through to the big hill without loss of momentum. The column got on the road at 0300; the distance to Objective 1 was six and a half miles. Had the weather stayed as moderate as during the Battalion's earlier operations, the march schedule would have entailed no excessive strain.

But they took off in a heavy snowstorm. There was little wind behind it, but it was a fine, powdery snow which already covered the ground to a depth of six to seven inches, made every step a partial skid and balled up thickly on the marchers' feet. By 0800, the Battalion had come to the nigh end of the big ridge and Charley Company was climbing to Objective 1. What had been a curse now became salvation. The snowfall had so thickened that visibility had been cut to less than seventy-five yards. In consequence, Charley Company seized the first knob without firing or receiving a shot, whereas otherwise the whole Battalion movement would have been under fire from the enemy main positions during the last 700 yards of the approach.

The 4.2 mortars were at once emplaced next to Objective 1. Three quad-50's and two twin-40's were run out to a side road which connected the MSR with a hydro-electric plant at the bottom of the gorge, and there aligned to fire against Hill 1081. By 1000, the main assault was underway, with Baker Company advancing astride the main road and Able pushing forward in file column along the knife-edged ridgeline, now ice-coated. The shooting started the moment Baker turned the next fold in the highway. But it was limited to spasmodic and erratic rifle fire from a few greatly surprised outposts. The storm still screened the attack from the main enemy positions along the higher ground. It was well so, since Baker was headed into a horseshoe-shaped battlement manned on three sides by enemy strength equivalent to one regiment. Approximately one battalion was bunkered-in along the upper knobs of Hill 1081. There were two strong roadblocks across the MSR just short of the hairpin turn. Another battalion was dug in on the far side of the gorge beyond the turn; and the transverse ridge which blocked the gorge and therefore dominated the hairpin turn was also crowned with enemy works.

Of these strong dispositions there was practically no sign as the Battalion advanced through the storm. Schmuck, remembering what he had seen of the Chinese in the open, knew about where he could expect to find them. But they had reacted so sluggishly that he already felt his plan had "achieved a tactical surprise which knocked them off balance."

Despite the initial thinness of the fire, Captain Wesley C. Noren and the men of Baker Company already had proof that they were in the presence of a numerous enemy. Along the road, the snow had been beaten down by hundreds of footprints, and the ridge slope was similarly marked as if a large force had moved in recent minutes to the peak. Baker came to the first Chinese roadblock. It was covered by the fire of two machine guns, but the fire pattern appeared to be mixed, either because the guns couldn't traverse or because the gunners couldn't see the targets through the storm. The beaten zones were interdicting the embankments and missing the road. The men watched for a few minutes, then climbed over the rubble and went on. Baker's own machine guns and 60-mm mortars were passed through the hoop, and then set up farther along the road at a point adjudged even with the enemy sites. By direct laying, the company's weapons silenced these guns, while still unable to see the ground whence the fire came. Its further fight with the roadblocks was almost an exact repetition of this incident.

Such was the celerity with which this initial maneuver along the road had been carried through that the battalion commander, following right on the heels of Baker Company, set up his CP in the sandbagged bunkers beside the first roadblock while it was still warm with the smell of the enemy. The occupants had fled without firing a shot, leaving behind two light machine guns, which were sited to fire straight down the canyon road. A kettle of rice was simmering on a small cook stove. One Chinese had been doing his laundry, and the abandoned garments were not only wet but warm. The bunkers were log revetted, backed up with rice bags filled with sand, the whole structure being neatly camouflaged with brush. The roof had an earth overhead thick enough to resist light artillery fire.

The 81-mm mortars were set up within ten feet of the CP at the closest point, and thence strung out along the upslope. This was a stricture which bedeviled the operation. Neither weapons nor vehicles were permitted to stand on the road surface—the only flat space available—because no one knew at what time the head of the 1st Marine Division column might appear or how fast the lead vehicles might be coming. The fact was that the road was still barred, the bridge not having been repaired, but for lack of information about the main body, Schmuck worked his own force under wraps.

Able Company, fighting forward amid the clouds, was harassed by no such major calculation. Among Captain Robert H. Barrow's men on the ridgetop, the problem was to find any spot where a weapon could be based or two men could stand abreast without danger of careening into the abyss. At Chinhung-ni that morning, they had started the march at 1200 feet above sea level. In the hour's climb to Charley's position they had reached 3000 feet, moving up a 45-degree slope. Already they felt giddy, and though they were not exhausted, they visibly sagged. Much of the way they had kept their footing only by forming a human chain. When that became necessary, the rifles were not only an impediment but a positive danger to the man forward and rear. Bruised skulls and sprained knees and ankles had been frequent.

From Charley's knob, Able proceeded slowly forward, moving Indian file. The ridge as it faced the road was almost sheer cliff, iced like a toboggan slide. The men moved bent

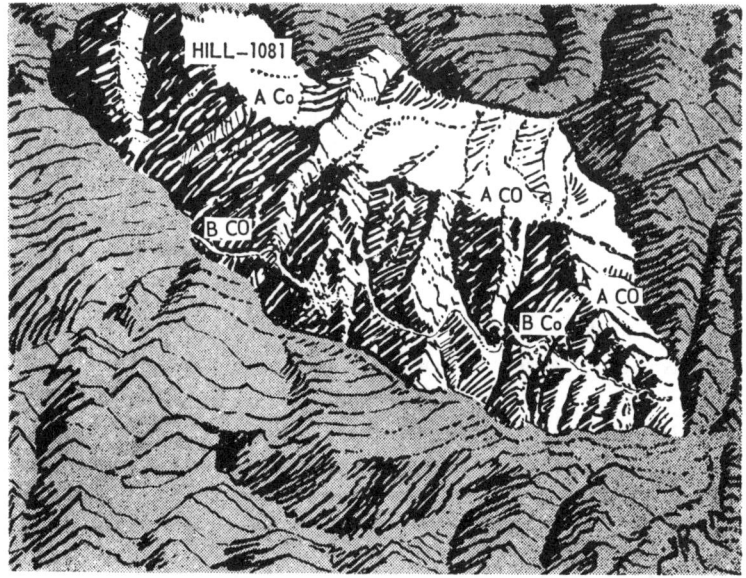

Two-Company Advance on Hill 1081

far over, grabbing for rocks or the occasional shrubs. Their first warning that the Chinese were on the crest occurred when they heard them talking and shouting somewhere out beyond the storm. Visibility came and went as the wind ripped holes in the snow curtain. Then for just a moment the snow ceased, and looking ahead, the company commander caught one brief glimpse of a group of enemy riflemen standing on a knob about 200 yards to his front. The curtain closed down so quickly that his own force went unobserved.

Hoping for another such respite, Captain Barrow brought his platoon leaders and the artillery and mortar forward observers forward, pointed into the storm and waited. But there was no slackening; the snow swirled more thickly than ever. So he attempted to bring in 4.2 fire by sound, figuring that he might follow it as it moved from the flank to across his front. One long try at this was enough. He could feel the ground shake around him but still could not see where the shells were exploding. So he knew it was time to drop the experiment.

He had already issued his attack order while the forward observers were attempting the adjustment, and he knew now that he would have to go forward without benefit of softening-up fires. Second Platoon led off, advancing like men walking a tight-rope. The narrow crest scarcely permitted one fire team to form abreast as they organized. It was a formation made formless by the desperate conditions of the ground. Men slithered along by ones or twos, forming a group front only as they emerged occasionally onto wider ground.

Right behind the Second Platoon came the 60-mm mortars. It was the intention to fire them, if the ground permitted at any point, like cannon, by direct laying. The Third Platoon followed. The First Platoon had been deployed in a partial perimeter around a knob to form a base.

There were three main knobs along the skyline, where the ridge folds joined, but unlike most Korean ridges, there were no flat saddles in between. These high points were all in enemy hands, and all were fitted with bunkers which both covered the road and faced down the ridgeline.

For perhaps seventy-five yards the lead files went along uninterrupted. Then automatic fire in heavy volume broke out against them. Men sought cover in the few crevices and behind the rocks, but the fire was consistently high, and the deployment paused only momentarily.

The men on the crest were told to go on "by fire and movement." In the tactical situation, it was a misnomer. Only one or two men could bound forward at a time; only a remnant could fire with a clear line to the target. Barrow knew he couldn't win that way. Either his men would land a hook on the enemy redoubt or the company would be jabbed to a standstill.

But it looked impossible; the embankments were as steep as they were thick. Two squads were told off to crawl along the left facing of the ridge, then come up and over; it was a task better suited to mountain goats than to men. On the right flank, two other squads were sent along a more favorable roundabout route, via which they could approach the enemy knob along a draw.

Such was the strain and danger of the movement because of the icing that it took a matter of hours to close this final 150 yards.

While the precarious envelopment proceeded, the 60-mm mortars were brought forward. They set up wherever crewmen could find a purchase so that the weapon could steady and the tube could bear on the target.

About one half-hour before dark, all things became ready. On both sides of the redoubt, the rifle and BAR men had crawled up to closing distance and lay in defilade behind the rocks. The mortars had been firing for about twenty minutes and altogether had loosed thirty rounds against the knob, though without getting one hit into the main bunkers.

Then from three sides Able closed all at once as the company commander gave the signal, the men on the flanks scrambling upward hand over foot, while the party on the crest bore straight forward with as much run as the footing allowed. It was bedlam, for in those last minutes the men remembered what Barrow had schooled them to do in training: "When you charge, yell with everything you got." Some screamed rebel yells. Others shouted, "Let's go!" and other things. They kept it up even when the ranks were thinned as men went down from bullets, and the dead or hard wounded skidded on down the incline.

The effect on the Chinese was startling. The knob suddenly came alive with people. They darted back and forth aimlessly as if unstrung by not finding a route out. Most of these targets in the open were cut down by machine-gun fire from the crest and the BAR's among the climbers.

But one hard core of resistance within the bunkers fired until the very last, and its members were eliminated by rifle fire and grenades through the embrasures. The hill had been strongly defended with grenades. But bullets had taken out most of the seven marine dead and eleven wounded, nearly all of whom were hit in the last rush. There were about threescore enemy dead in and around the bunkers.

Noren & Company, during these hours, had been proceeding with their work along the MSR. They had expected to receive fire from the far side of the hairpin turn, and they got it, mainly from machine guns, in the moments when the snowfall abated. But it, too, was inflexible, as if parts of the guns were frozen. The third enemy roadblock was the most tenacious of the three. But the ground was such that Baker could maneuver against it, despite the steepness of the embankment. For the third time that day, the company commander used both his 60-mm mortars and 3.5 launchers against the Chinese bunkers without having any luck. The position was not squeezed out until riflemen were put on its rear, and then rushed the works; only three Chinese chose to die beside their weapons; the rest got away down the gorge.

That happened at about 1630. Captain Noren was becoming concerned about his objective. He knew he was close to it, but couldn't be sure of the spot because the snowdrifts made identification almost impossible. By then Baker had lost three men killed and six wounded. The battalion commander, checking the situation aloft and below, told both companies to dig in and hold for the night. But the ground all around was pitted with enemy diggings, and that was a bonus, for both outfits were now well worn.

Noren picked out a subridge about 200 yards up the slope. As a measure of the fight with the rocks and the weather, it took the main body one hour to climb to the perimeter ground. The company also set up two roadblocks along the MSR to halt any enemy movement toward the south. Able had set up around the enemy redoubt on the skyline.

Nothing had come down from Koto-ri and the division's progress could be only guessed at.

The Battalion was to spend one more bad night and another good day before the sight of a sea of friendly faces marked the completion of its mission.

Last Barrier II

At dark on 8 December, the snowfall ceased and the cold intensified. Down along the canyon road near the water gate, a brisk wind was piling the drifts as high as a man's head.

At the Battalion CP, which was partly sheltered by the canyon wall, the thermometer read thirty degrees below zero. Up on the windswept crags where Able Company was clearing Chinese dead from the bunkers to make room for its own ranks, and at the same time preparing to evacuate its own casualties down the iced slopes of the mountain, it must have been a touch colder than that, though there was no reading of the temperature.

All batteries had frozen. Weapons were stiffening. The camp long since had run out of water because of the freezing of canteens. To ease their thirst, the men ate snow and seemed to thrive on it.

But of the many problems raised by the weather, the most severe one was getting an average good man to observe what the field manuals so easily describe as a "common sense precaution."

For example, prior to marching from Chinhung-ni, Captain Barrow of Able had made certain that each of his men carried two spare pairs of socks. But that safeguard did not of itself insure his force, though the men, with feet sweated from the rigors of the day, were all at the point of becoming frostbite casualties by the hour of bivouac.

Let Barrow tell it. "I learned that night that only leadership will save men under winter conditions. It's easy to say that men should change socks; getting it done is another matter. Boot laces become iced over during prolonged engagements in snowdrifts. It's a fight to get a boot off the foot. When a man removes his gloves to struggle with the laces, it seems to him that his hands are freezing. His impulse is all against it. So I found it necessary to do this by order, staying with the individuals until they had changed, then making them get up and move about to restore the circulation."

That process, simple in the telling, consumed hours. By the time Barrow was satisfied that his command was relatively snug, it was wearing on toward midnight. Right then, his perimeter was hit by a counterattack, an enemy force in platoon-strength-plus striking along the ridgeline from 1081 in approximately the same formation which Barrow had used during the afternoon.

All that needs be told about this small action is summed up in Barrow's brief radio report to Schmuck. "They hit us. We killed them all—all that we could see. We have counted eighteen fresh bodies just outside our lines."

This was the lesser activity of the night, the greater being the evacuation of Able's casualties to the low ground. It was a man-killing task, conducted round the clock. Battalion had detailed the men of Headquarters & Supply Company, with a complement from Weapons Company, to this duty. They walked singly going up, carrying ammunition, and despite the glaciated condition of the slope, they made the climb in about one and one-half hours. But for the descent, they now had to group in relay teams of eight men each, just to handle one body in a litter. Without ropes, it would have been impossible. Sometimes they were needed to tie the party together; at other points, they were used to lower the litter down an iced bank where no man could stand.

The downward journey for each evacuation required from

five to seven hours. The Battalion had a forward aid station just behind its CP, and a rear at Chinhung-ni, each under a Battalion surgeon. Motors were kept running through the night so that casualties could be speeded to the base.

The plain recital of these difficulties, however, does not begin to reflect the extraordinary hazards of the situation. The First Battalion was encamped cheek-by-jowl next to a vastly superior enemy force which had not yet begun to feel the pressure of the division driving down from the north. There was nothing to prevent the Chinese from swinging around the left via the canyon floor and closing across its rear, but the Battalion had to remain committed to the heights if it was to accomplish its mission of safeguarding the division's passage through the worst deadfall along its route out.

Though Battalion had given a brilliant account of itself throughout the fight, as things looked on the night of 8 December, its main hope of delivering the package according to plan was that the enemy would suffer even more direly from the one adversary against which they were mutually contending. Even though Schmuck's own people were near to freezing, and in the operations of that night he was to lose sixty-seven men to frostbite (only six or seven became amputees) the weather simply had to be on his side. The main chance was that the weather would produce greater immobility in the enemy camp than in the Marines'. Already, in repeated situations, the division had won through because, while the enemy brutally wasted his manpower against the weather, General Smith missed no opportunity to conserve the powers of his men. The deliberate rest periods given the division on its way out are among the salient lessons attending the success of the operation.

But the tactical and human risks still to be faced were but one-half the jeopardy. There was the other great question of whether the technical and materiel calculations would prove sound. The Battalion was only standing guard on a peak 1500 yards distant; the breach at the water gate still had to be spanned if the division was to get through the canyon with anything left save numbers of men.

Bad luck in the handling of this bottleneck had dogged the operation from the beginning. But no one looked the other way. In fact, the division's continuing concern with this relatively small fester on its rear gives increased breadth to the maxim that anticipation is 70 per cent of the art of command.

Going up the mountain, Colonel John H. Partridge had recognized that the bridge was a weak link in the MSR chain if winter operations were to be sustained, and had reenforced the structure to fifty-ton strength. A day or two later it was partly demolished, either by guerrillas or the Chinese Communist Forces.

Meanwhile the 73rd Engineer Battalion of X Corps had taken over maintenance of the MSR. They put two sections of steel treadway across the gap and the road was again whole.

Then the Communists struck it again. On 4 December, a reconnaissance flight into the canyon verified that the bridge was blown, the treadway sections had been dropped and the abutment on the downhill side had been partly destroyed. The gap was estimated at eighteen feet.

General Smith suggested that a Bailey bridge be brought up the mountain by corps troops, and emplaced by his own engineers as they moved south in the van of the division. Partridge and his staff returned the answer that the roadway was too narrow at that point to support a Bailey.

By chance the 58th Treadway Bridge Company had been caught at Koto-ri when the CCF attack struck on 28 November. It had the necessary Brockway trucks but no bridging material, the vehicles being loaded with prefabricated housing intended to shelter the Corps CP when it set up in Hagaru-ri.

The request was sent to Hamhung: have a bridge air-dropped on Koto-ri; for double insurance, the First Engineer Battalion was asked to proceed from that point up the mountain with a duplicate set of treadway material.

The siege at Koto-ri had also closed on the 185th Engineer Battalion. Its commander was directed to beat the camp for all lumber and other materials which might be used for bridging and to make ready the equipment of the Treadway Company, his attachment.

On 6 December, Colonel Partridge was flown down over the water gate so that he could personally survey the problem. Returning to Koto-ri, he called Hamhung and was told that a test drop of the bridge had damaged its parts beyond repair. But a specialist parachute rigger was already flying from Japan. He would re-rig with large chutes eight pieces of a treadway which would be dropped on Koto-ri on the morning of 7 December.

They came in on schedule, eight C-119's, carrying the eight bridge sections, center plywood section, pins, etc. Seven of the sections were retrieved, the eighth falling into enemy country. Two of the four plywood sections were salvageable.

The bridge was loaded with its essential pieces on one Brockway truck, the spare pieces and extra lumber aboard a second. This unit was then fitted into the plan for the attack by the 7th Marines so that it would be well forward.

On the morning of 8 December, it stood by briefly. At noon the forward battalion of the 7th Marines sent word that the situation was in hand and the bridge could roll. Its arrival amid the attacking battalion coincided with the highest pitch of the snowstorm and a reborn fury in the enemy resistance. Mortar and small-arms fire threatened the destruction of the entire hope.

The two Brockways were withdrawn to Colonel Homer Litzenberg's 7th Regiment CP. There was a convenient flat space near his tent which had been used for parking lighter vehicles. The bridge-loaded trucks cut off the road into this area. But the flat space was the frozen surface of a lake. One Brockway broke through the ice, drowned its motor and damaged its radiator. The other Brockway and a pack of jeeps were used to tug it out.

That was enough for Litzenberg. He directed that because of "the tactical situation," the bridge unit be returned to Koto-ri. But because of the dark, the depth of the drifts and the fact that one Brockway was towing the other, they got no farther than the tank park just to the rear of the regimental CP.

After this record of adversity and mishap, in which fate had so consistently balked the best-laid plans that the play would have seemed comic had the stakes been less, there was no longer any margin for error.

In the next turn of the wheel, the right number had to come up, and no doubt about it.

Schmuck had to hold.

The bridge had to fit.

Partridge's long-range estimate of the requirement had to match the exact need on the spot.

Either this, or the entire plan for bringing out the division as a whole would dissolve at the fatal gap.

But on the night of 8-9 December, there was no way of knowing. The die had been cast and men could only hope.

The morning dawned sunny, absolutely clear and terribly cold. Captain Barrow, taking his first view of the weather, concluded that he would get full help from supporting arms, and particularly from the air.

Moving among the platoons, he ordered an immediate test firing of all weapons. It was well so, for about 40 per cent of all small arms had frozen, with the carbines and BAR's giving the worst trouble. Down at the Battalion CP they heard the volleying from this freezing exercise and Major Bridges called to inquire: "Are you being counterattacked?"

Barrow answered that his bullets weren't being wasted. The dome of Hill 1081 glistened in the sun just 500 yards away, and over its surface the Chinese swarmed like a bed of ants on moving day. The machine guns had pointed that way for their warm-up fires. Two or three of the enemy were felled by this automatic volley, but the others paid little heed. At that range the gunners could not see where the bullets were hitting. So Able's CO put his riflemen against the target and under pressure of the aimed fire, the Chinese slowly beat back to their earth holes. By the time the light mortars along the ridge and the heavies from the Battalion position had joined the action, it was too late to catch any important number of the Chinese in the open. Point 1081 looked almost depopulated, as did the intervening portion of the hogback.

Able Company expected to encounter little trouble as it jumped off in the same formation as the day before, with First Platoon in the assault, followed by Third Platoon and then the mortars. But immediately the squad working along the slope on the right flank came under direct fire from two machine guns on Hill 1081 and had to take refuge behind the rocks. Barrow saw clearly enough that their way was barred and, adding a light machine-gun section to the flank, directed the men to continue their fire against the main knob.

Meanwhile the squad working along the left slope in relative defilade had made rapid progress. Gaining to within 200 yards of the big knob, it was suddenly brought under machine-gun fire from its direct right. At a hitherto concealed position, the CCF were holding two bunkers in a saddle about 175 yards short of Hill 1081. From behind rock cover, the squad engaged this block with rifles and BAR's, firing steadily but making no effort to rush. While the diversion continued, a third squad was sent on a wider sweep along the same flank, and coming at the bunkers from their blind side (still without being observed from 1081), killed the inmates with grenades and rifle fire in a closing rush without losing one man.

Able now held the whole ridge except for 1081. Almost within throwing distance, it towered seventy-five feet above the saddle which Able had just gained. The 60-mm mortars were advanced to the rocky battlement from behind which the LMG's had been firing, and fired forty-three rounds against the big knob, which was all they had. There was no noticeable effect, other than that the automatic fire from the height was temporarily depressed, enabling Captain Barrow to get his two assault platoons forward on both sides of the ridgeline, until they were deployed in an arc around the final objective, 150 yards from the summit. From behind crag cover, the riflemen maintained a steady fire against the peak. Such was the perspective that even at this short distance the bunker embrasures looked like a hairline.

That was when the air was brought in. Captain Robert B. Robinson, Schmuck's air officer, had been with Able through the morning, and from the boulder-strewn knob just to rearward of the two platoons had witnessed their squeeze play against the last redoubt. The 60-mms had put a few smoke rounds on the summit just as a precaution, though its mass was almost unmistakable. Already orbiting, the four aircraft were under control by Robinson via a back-packed radio. They followed SOP. First there was a dummy run, then a quick strafing pass to make sure they were exactly on target. Thereafter it was up to the flight leader to make his own runs in the direction indicated, and drop his bombs and rockets with no further corrections from the ground unless he got off target.

Directly atop 1081 there was a double telephone pole— the perfect aiming stake. Each plane made five passes. The air officer was just 200 yards away while he was calling the strike, and the closest men in Able's line halved that distance. They saw several of the 265-pound frag bombs land dead on, smashing two of the bunkers and killing their crews. As the smoke lifted, one Chinese jumped up in clear silhouette and turned to run from the hill. Rifle fire cut him down before he could take a stride.

In the middle of the strike, Able Company had been moving. First Platoon, on the left flank, displaced once again down the westward slope, and made a circuit halfway around 1081, so that when it emerged once again on the skyline, it was approaching the redoubt from the north. For the first time during the operation, it had the advantage of good tree and underbrush cover as it made the swing around. During this envelopment, the men still confronting 1081 did not cease fire, but in keeping with the maneuver, shifted their line more and more to the right.

So they were all ready for the final play, and right then occurred one of those happy accidents of timing which so frequently build the fortunes of men who are willing to make their own luck in battle. As First Platoon came out on the skyline, some one of its members happened to glance out northwestward toward the Koto-ri road. Some-one yelled: "Look! There comes the division!" True enough they could be seen now, perhaps a dozen men turning the bend in the road on the far side of the canyon, obviously the point of the 7th Regiment in the van of the division column. Others took up the cry; it was the only spur the attack needed; all hands knew that 1081 had to be taken and the Chinese cleared from every other point whence they could fire toward the wrecked bridge before the division main body began the descent into the defile.

First Platoon bounded toward the cap and, once in motion, slackened its pace only as the detail of hitting or being hit so required. It was no push-over. On the reverse slope, where the air had struck, the Chinese responded numbly to Third Platoon's fire. Had it been done at once, the hill might have been carried more easily from that side, but the other maneuver was already two-thirds complete and to counter-mand it would have wrought only confusion. So there was no choice but to continue on the hard way.

Upgrade perhaps thirty feet or so, two bunkers were directly athwart First Platoon's path. No machine guns here, but only rifles, sub-machine guns, and potato mashers, with both ports still blazing and the grenades showering down seemingly out of nowhere. Seven or eight of Able's men went down; the survivors rushed straight for the embrasures and killed the bunkers by tossing in their last grenades. Not one Chinese made any attempt to surrender, though perhaps twenty of them were shot down in the open as they arose from among the rocks on both sides of the bunkers in an effort to break the charge with small arms fire. Subsequent examination showed that the majority of them had been armed with U.S. carbines.

The fight was not yet over. First Platoon had silenced only an outwork of the north slope position. From this minor terrace the men saw a line of four bunkers another thirty yards upslope. Until then masked to their sight, these positions had remained in defilade to the fires put against the cap from both directions.

There was only one visible source of resupply for this job. Dead Chinese littered the ground just taken. In each bunker (these installations were five feet deep in the ground, log-walled and with an eighteen-inch earth roof) there were about seven or eight enemy dead. Most of these figures still had a few potato mashers slung in their belts. While First Platoon collected the enemy grenades, a reenforcement from Third Platoon crept around 1081 to build up the pressure against the bunker line by fire and grenading from the flanks.

This closing scene was handled a little more deliberately and stealthily. Using rock cover, the Marine line simply made it a squeeze-out, the rifles and the BAR's keeping the bunker line practically neutralized until the grenadiers could crawl forward to within killing range. In another half-hour it was over. No Chinese had gotten away from Hill 1081. But it had been a tenacious garrison and not one member of it survived to tell how things had been with the defender.

Those who saw this ruin under the noonday sun recalled most vividly its startling contrast. For as far as eye could see the countryside wore a white blanket. But the de-iced and shattered cap of Hill 1081 had been burned black by the shelling and bombfire. Within the boundaries of this torched area, the victors counted more than 300 Chinese bodies.

Down in the canyon, however, the situation was still in flux, and though the linch-pin of the general position was gone, enemy bands were continuing a disorganized resistance. Whereas Barrow's problem was the relatively simple one of loosing a battering ram against a brick wall, Noren was pressed to find anything solid on which to crunch. There were Chinese all about him but they were peculiarly elusive.

Baker's night had been quiet, only one Chinese having blundered into his lines. But Captain Noren, awake at his post all night, saw no bright omen in that fact. He said to the others: "Wait till dawn and you'll see them swarming." First light confirmed his powers as a prophet. He glanced up the road, and to the ridges beyond; the vista was alive with people, but there was no pattern to what they were doing; most of them were milling about in small groups, and at least half seemed to be unarmed. This was the beginning of the backwash from the division's drive out of Koto-ri, the trapper recoiling into his own trap.

That quick look also showed Noren that in the dark of the previous evening he had missed his proper objective by one ridge fold, and was not in position to cover the hairpin turn. Baker Company corrected that by banging ahead immediately, re-establishing its weapons right on the pivot.

Even this brief movement showed who was master. Instead of concentrating toward the thrust, the Chinese gave way, scampering toward the high ground east and west.

Baker Company had already registered its supporting 105's on the ridges ahead, and found their fire so erratic that Noren hesitated to use it. (This is a not infrequent entry in the Reservoir operation.) Communications with the 4.2-mm and 81-mm mortars were out, and were not re-established until mid-morning. So Baker went pot-shooting with the 155-mm howitzers as a man might bang away at quail with a scatter gun. Consistently, the shells came in exactly where Noren wanted them. So he kept calling the 155's to chase Chinese up and down the road and blast them from the ridge tops. Concurrently his own machine guns and rifles at the bend of the hairpin were chopping down an incoherent mass not more than 200 yards away—Chinese trying without plan or leader to break through along the road. It was an act of utter hysteria.

As the morning wore along, these signs of mass frenzy increased. Buffeted by the point of 7th Regiment pushing down from Koto-ri, finding no thoroughfare via the canyon road, these increments succumbed emotionally to the vestiges of an entrapment not even half-formed. Schmuck, who watched this phenomenon develop, said of it: "The column flushed them into our foreground as beaters drive birds into a blind. All day it went on. Noren had a clear view of the whole slot and put the mortars and artillery on them when they were beyond range of company weapons. If they tried to escape eastward over the ridges, they came under Barrow's fire from 1081, or were hit by air strikes called in by Robinson. From the high ground northward of us, they could range in on our lines with mortars and machine guns. But they were too panic-stricken to settle and so their fire went wild. Charley Company had extended to the westward along the east-west ridge to tie in with Able; that strengthened our command of the high ground. From our part of the road, the quad-50's were in perfect position to bring down what the other weapons missed."

At noontime came the first brief interlude in this ordeal

of carnage. From the heights, at a decisive moment, Barrow had seen the point of 7th Regiment during the approach. The battalion commander witnessed the same group of riflemen as they began their descent into the canyon. There was one excited moment of waving and yelling across the far spaces. But the new entry was only a small patrol from Baker Company, 7th. Chinese hidden in a thicket directly across the canyon from the battalion CP brought them under fire. In a flash they had vanished, at least from Schmuck's ken. But Noren had a better view of the incident. He saw a CCF machine gun open fire on the patrol. He saw seven Marines attack up the hill behind the fire of one BAR. He saw the seven go into the thicket throwing grenades, and when they came out a few minutes later the machine gun was silent, and the seven still seemed to be all right. Then the patrol was lost to sight. Some time later they entered Schmuck's lines, helping along five walking wounded. Quitting the road, they had reached home base via a circuitous route through the canyon.

Using the patrol's radio, Schmuck raised First Battalion, 7th. But the van of the column was still some distance away.

With the coming of twilight, the enemy numbers suddenly thickened. The new bands seemed better organized and proceeded to positions astride the inclined railway and confronting the hairpin turn. Guns and tubes were running short of ammunition. So Schmuck called for an air strike and eight planes responded to give him the best show of the day. One 500-pound bomb exploded dead center on a large building that was packed with Chinese. The others strafed liberally up and down the tracks and blasted the buildup with a rain of rockets.

Still the numbers grew. When shortly afterward, Schmuck got a call from First Battalion, 7th, with the message: "We're about to come through," he answered, "My God, don't do it! Half the road is still held by Chinese." The reply was final: "Can't help it; the pressure is on from the rear."

At that point, perhaps, Schmuck was being a little unrealistic. The mobile Brockway carrying the treadway (the damaged vehicle had proved such a hindrance that it had been left behind) had already reached the water gate under heavy escort and the bridging operation had been going on for several hours amid all the fire. A quick survey showed that additional demolitions had now widened the gap between solid abutments to twenty-nine feet. The solution recommended on the spot was to build on the downhill side a cribbing structure which would narrow the gap to dimensions suitable for the treadway. The engineeers had not brought forward enough material for this job, but they quickly prowled the hydroelectric plant and came up with what they needed. By late afternoon the bridge looked stout enough to withstand the column's passage. The engineers sent word to the tactical body to come on down the mountain.

The main body and vehicles of First Battalion, 7th, crossed the bridge first and entered Baker's position about 2300. The Chinese who were still confronting Baker took a few half-hearted shots at the approaching line and then came in with their hands up—300 of them. "Buzz" Sawyer, the battalion commander, passed the prize over to Baker Company, which later marched them down the hill to Chinhungni, whence they were escorted to the coast by elements of 3d Infantry Division.

This was the beginning of the long march-through which kept Able and Baker tied to their snow-banked diggings through all the next day.

Again on this night the enemy crumpled to the attack by the cold and made no effort to harass the column's passage. But disaster of quite another sort threatened just as the movement got well underway. A TD18 engineer dozer hauling an eight-cubic-yard pan started across the bridge.

The Water Gap—Most Dangerous Defile in Korea

The treadways in construction had been spread for use by the M26 tank; and the plywood center section, suspended on a tracer bar, was thought to be capable of sustaining all weights and treads other than the M26. But the plywood centerway collapsed under the weight of the dozer, and one treadway track went down. That left the tractor suspended in midair, and to the eyes of the engineers it looked as though the bridge was ruined beyond repair.

Technical Sergeant Prosser mounted the dozer atop the tottering structure, and by some magic which the others never understood, managed to manipulate it back onto solid earth. The plywood centerway was removed and the failed spacers taken out. Then by the sweat of many men and ingenious use of the tractor blade—it being employed as a lever—the treadways were put back into position. All of this was done in darkness except as the feeble glow of a few flashlights assisted the operation. Hundreds of men were milling around on the nigh side of the gap, including fifty Chinese prisoners who had chosen this hour to surrender. The flashlight wielders had to stay there through the night so that the now malformed treadway could be illuminated.

When first light arrived, the column began to receive small arms fire from the draw where the inclined railway cut out to the northeastward. Schmuck told Baker Company to get a patrol up there and stop the racket. Two squads went along reenforced with a 3.5 rocket team. They quickly located the Chinese in two stoutly formed bunkers, halfway up the ridge. The first was knocked out with four rounds from the launcher. The second was too well-fronted with brush for the rockets to cut through. The rifle squads took it with fire and movement, using hand grenades at the finish. Four Chinese were killed, two surrendered, four got away. Each nest had contained one machine gun. The patrol got back with only two men slightly wounded.

That was the final skirmish around the water gate. It took the division column twenty-eight hours to pass through Baker's roadblock. When at last the tank battalion cleared, Schmuck ordered Barrow to come down from his icy hilltop. The dead came out with the living. The score was counted: total losses were forty-seven killed and wounded and 190 casualties of the cold. Schmuck also checked his other list on which he had kept tab of the division units passing through: it was complete.

But still they tarried. Streams of refugees were coming down the ridges trying to escape the Chinese; all converged on the treadway bridge. Thrice a charge of 800 pounds of Composition C placed under the span had been at the point of detonation, and thrice the blast had been deferred to accommodate the wayfarers. Finally the road cleared, and at 0200 on 11 December, CWO Willie S. Harrison blew the bridge.

Schmuck formed the Battalion and accompanied the armor down the mountain. As he expressed it, they were delighted with one another's company.

All hands could then look back over the road traveled and reflect with understanding on the words of the division commander: "Not even Genghis Khan would have put an army across these mountains in the wintertime."

THE FIGHT ON SAKI NIGHT

How It All Started

I am not sure *The Fight on Saki Night* belongs in this medley. Herein I have attempted to collect the most unusual and instructive combat stories with which I have personally been identified in one capacity or another. The last real fight on Makin Island is in a twilight zone. The reactions of the men in the fire line were as eccentric and informative as are to be expected of soldiers of any land in a small unit action. On the other hand, it was not in any real sense an exemplary operation in that the troops were never under discriminating control and in the circumstances of the night, it was impossible for them so to be. For this condition, it is not possible to attach blame to anyone. I had been with them through that day. We had marched through most of it under a boiling equatorial sun, supposedly in the presence of the enemy, though we heard scarcely a shot fired. The heat got to everyone. When sundown came and we had to go into perimeter, there was hardly a man present who was still capable of functioning and of insisting on the doing of what Field Service Regulations required. Certainly I was not; I was clean forspent, to borrow a phrase from the Bible. Throughout the late afternoon I had watched these men, and despite my own distrait condition of mind at the time, I retained an indelible impression of them. It seemed a miracle to me that they could keep going on. Their jaws were down and seemed to be sunken almost to their chests. There was a yellowish spittle around the lips which is always seen in fighting men when they are not only parched but in a state of extreme exhaustion. After this condition is reached, it is idle and wasteful to push troops. Nothing good is to be expected of them. But these men had to be pushed by their battalion commander. They had been given orders, and the orders were there to be executed. It was deplorable but the whole thing was as simple as that.

Here I must recapitulate. When the historical operation of World War II was first begun, there were only three of us, Lieutenant Colonel John Mason Kemper, Lieutenant Colonel Charles Taylor and myself. In our first conversations in a small cubbyhole atop the Pentagon, we talked as equal numbers about how to solve the vast problems which lay ahead of us and had almost without warning or instruction been dropped in our laps. Most of that discussion is not germane to this memorandum. But when we turned to the subject of what we would undertake to cover, my two colleagues were of the view that we would have to forget first-hand reporting of combat operations because we had come too late to the problem and our resources promised to be too little for that. To this I vehemently objected. My argument was that if we did not know how our men performed in battle, all the rest of it would be superficial. The test of America at war lay in the effectiveness of the hands on the combat line and not in how various headquarters interpreted what they were doing. Kemper and Taylor were sympathetic to this view; they simply doubted that we could stretch that far. However, I was insistent and when at a later date the Operations Division nixed the paper by which we sought a right-of-way and an official blessing on access to the combat line and to dealing with the high command on all aspects of decision-making, I said to Kemper: "We will have to get this overridden by the Chief of Staff's office or we might as well go out of business." Johnny was game. He went immediately to General Joseph McNarney, who was sitting in for George C. Marshall, and in a five-minute conversation, he won us our charter. It is impossible to give this one individual too much credit for the success of World War II Historical Operations. With a less resolute boss, relatively little would have been accomplished by anyone.

Now it had been more or less assumed from the beginning that I would be the main wheel at home base in the Pentagon, since I was the only editor and writer so far identified with the operation. I was perfectly content to leave it that way, having no desire for further combat service. But in our early conversations I had said to Kemper that I was wholly dissatisfied with military history as we had read it up until that point, since it almost invariably led to a dead-end where guessing and romance took over. Always the "fog of war" intervened at the most crucial point of the fighting and what happened thereafter had to be determined by guess and by God. I felt sure that there must be available some better system for the collecting of combat information, if men were but sharp enough to recognize it. Kemper agreed with my reasoning. Further he deployed himself to the Kiska Operation to seek that "better system" which we had agreed could become the heart of our operation. But as everyone knows, Kiska turned out to be a dry-run operation with no enemy present and I received from him a classic cable on his disappointment: "This is the last of my Aleutians." After his return he realized that I was the only man in the show who had been in combat, who had dealt with higher field headquarters in time of war and whose name was known to the greater number of our high commanders overseas. So he decided on his own that I would have to be the field man.

He called me in one day and asked: "Sam, would you like to have overseas service?"

I replied: "No."

He said: "I don't understand your answer."

I said: "All right then, John, I will spell it out for you. No!"

He said: "I have never heard of a General Staff officer returning such an answer to that question."

I said: "John, that's only because I haven't been asked before."

He said: "I still don't get it."

I said: "John, in that case I'll parse it for you. If you have a tough order that you wish to give me, then you give it to me straight out! If you asked me whether I wanted duty in the ZI, I'd still say *No.* I don't particularly want anything. But don't ask me to relieve your mind and your conscience by trying to give me what you are attempting to force me to say I want. A commander doesn't act that way. You give me an order and I'll comply. But if I get overseas and you don't support me to the limit I'll burn your tail until you'll never be able to sit again."

This wonderful West Pointer, as resilient a chief as I have ever known in army life or anywhere else, first laughed like a fool and then said: "Okay, I've had my lesson. I'll never make that mistake again." It was never necessary to burn his tail; he was always the soul of consideration and appropriate response.

Shortly I got my orders. They were as ambiguous and as generalized as if they had been written by a file clerk. That was not Kemper's fault. It was due to the hyper-caution of our security methodology in the Pentagon under G-2. This is not the appropriate place to discuss the difficulties in detail. Suffice to say that dealing with a General Staff in wartime is trouble enough when adult males behave normally instead of carrying out their functions like small children.

In due course, after a few misadventures, I found myself at Makin Island in the Gilberts dealing with the 27th Infantry Division, or more specifically with its God-fearing commander, that gentlemanly gentleman, my good friend Major General Ralph Smith. Only one small portion of his command participated in the first invasion out of Central Pacific operations, that of the RCT of the 165th Infantry (formerly the Fighting 69th of New York) and some attached units. They have been heavily libeled in the years since but I remember them as boon companions, joyous company in a frolic and worthy of their uniforms during a fight.

It was a custom in the Central Pacific to give any attached General Staff officer an additional duty beyond the specialty which brought about his assignment. I have always felt that this idea is perfectly sound because it is quite likely that a specific mission may be thwarted for reasons beyond control of the individual and therefore he is likely to become either a goldbrick or, what is worse, a mere sightseer. My job was to look for that "new system." Ralph Smith called me in and told me that the extra task was to become responsible for bringing off an increased capture of enemy prisoners of war, which in the case of the Japanese was no sinecure, besides which I hadn't the foggiest notion of how to proceed, having come too late to the Pacific area.

During the first two days of battle, I didn't worry about it. My hands were more than full, and worse yet, I got nowhere. The battle was too close-joined even to think about bringing off Japanese surrenders. It was hard enough to get a bead on the enemy and kill him. But in these two days I did my utmost to find that "new system." I dealt with officers, NCO's and privates either in the combat line or fresh out of it. What they said I recorded in my notes, but the notes were worthless. They were a hodge-podge of hallucination and phantasmagoria. Every witness spoke in hyperbole. Each man's statement contradicted what some other man had said. At the end of the two days I felt wholly defeated and wired Kemper: "There is no system and no possibility of finding one. The mission is a failure."

With that done, I felt I was free to set forth on my other chore. The battle had become more fluid. Such of the enemy as remained on Makin Island had seemingly faded back into the scenery. I recall Major General Holland M. Smith, the corps commander from the Marines, going to General Ralph

Smith and saying to him: "Get your men out. What's holding you up? There's not another goddammed Jap on this island."

So the Third Battalion of the 165th slogged along through that afternoon on a rout march which was supposed to take it to the extreme tip of Makin. I rode in a jeep through the early part of the day, which is mentioned because of an unforgettable experience. Aboard the vehicle with me was a character named Willie whose last name I have long since forgotten. He was about twenty-two years old and a native son of Makin. When the Japanese first invaded that island, Willie had shoved off in a small boat and crossed a broad stretch of the Pacific to one of the British possessions, this to escape capture. He had then become a member of the Fiji Scouts. When we prepared to invade Makin the United States Army borrowed him because of his knowledge of the Gilberts. Willie's father lived on the island and when last seen by Willie was about to pass into Japanese captivity. Willie had heard nothing from him since. So as the Japanese fell back (if there were any left) we were in the act of carrying Willie to a sentimental rendezvous. I imagined it would be something like Stanley greeting Dr. Livingstone in the heart of Africa, and in fact that was how it turned out to be, because as history records, when Stanley said: "Dr. Livingstone, I presume." the great man answered only: "Yes." So it was with Willie despite our high anticipations. When we at last got to the little shack which was the family domicile, an old man came walking down the garden path through the smoke which cloaked the environs. He looked at his son and said: "Willie." Willie looked at him and said: "Pa!" That was it. They did not embrace. Nor did they show the slightest sign of emotion. We left them there both acting like ships which pass in the night.

The confused fight of that night is as described in the narrative which follows. It was not a brilliant action. But may I say that I have never dealt with troops in a night action who knew less of what had happened when morning came. I was there with my Nisei interpreter, Corporal Kubo, and a jeep-loaded radio loudspeaker to attempt bringing about surrenders at the time when the scene cooled and the Japanese once again retreated into the landscape. What the battalion had been through was beyond guessing. Before we had gotten out of our tracks I had heard three or four stories about one soldier who had been run through with a Japanese saber amid the perils of the night. It never occurred to me or to anyone else that there may have been more than one American in the line who had been thus skewered. The same is true of all other personal incidents. Via the grapevine we had three or four accounts of each before we could get started.

But the mission remained the same. Third Battalion had to go to the end of the island, clearing the last ground in the liberation of Makin. We marched via a sand-surfaced road which ran along the edge of the lagoon and although we started at eight o'clock, it was almost noon before we reached the end of the coral. As we walked along I said to the Battalion commander, my red-haired friend, Joe Hart: "If in some way I can find out what happened to this battalion last night, I feel sure that I can clarify any tactical situation in war; the whole thing was like a nightmare; it couldn't happen." Joe replied: "I agree with you. I haven't the slightest idea what happened to my men. That one last night is just about as confused as they come."

The key to the story was unquestionably the platoon which had held its ground in the center and the one machine gun which had continued to fire in its defense. There was no other obvious starting point. So when we got to the end of the island, and most of the men prepared to cool their tootsies in the blue water, I sent for Murray, the platoon commander, and Schwartz, the man who had been on the gun. My purpose was to talk things over with them briefly and personally so that I might know where to start later.

Murray arrived first and we talked. He reached the point where he said to me: "So when I knew that the gun crew was knocked out, I ordered Schwartz to go forward and take it over." From behind the palm tree next which I was sitting came a voice saying: "Oh, no you didn't, Lieutenant. You didn't do any such thing. I was 30 yards from you in a fox-hole by myself. I heard you shout to the men that the gun was gone and the platoon should fix bayonets and prepare to meet the Japs as they came on. I knew that if we did that the whole Battalion would be overrun. So I crawled forward and took over the gun without anybody ordering me."

I do not recall clearly how Murray reacted. In any case I do not doubt his good faith or his conviction that he was speaking truthfully. Men under the strain of battle very often forget what they have said or done and much evil comes of these aberrations. But the discrepancy was so great that there could be no reconciling the two statements. Later on I formed all of the survivors of the platoon that I might hear from other witnesses. There seemed only one logical way to bring about clarification. I told Murray to start at the beginning and describe how he had placed his men and what orders he had given them. I said that from that lead we would try to take up step by step what each member of the platoon had done or said and that I would be responsible for seeing that we maintained a chronological order.

What came forth was not unlike the story of the fool for luck who falls in a sewer and comes up with a diamond ring. Not only did we determine the truth as between Schwartz and Murray, but by the end we knew everything that had happened to this platoon despite the confusions of the night.

In this way a new process was born. It was not that I discovered it; it discovered me. Truth does indeed arise out of the dust; but there should be added that it needs hit one between the eyes several times before one sees it. It is of no moment that thereafter one may receive undeserved credit for great cleverness. What I had learned from the platoon, I next applied to the Battalion as a whole and then to the 165th Regiment. When we invaded the Marshall Islands a little more than two months later, I applied it to the entire 7th Infantry Division, which big-scale experiment was made easy by the vision and active support of Major General Archibald Arnold.

So I knew before I ever went to the European Theatre at the time of Normandy what we ought to do there. The system continued to work faultlessly wherever we applied it. But it could not be expanded to cover all of the combat operations in ETO because our count of officers and NCO's who could carry out such field word effectively was far too small.

The Fight on Saki Night I

THE conquest of Makin Island in November, 1943, was so far overshadowed by the nearby Battle of Tarawa that today that other target in the Gilberts is all but forgotten.

Such fleeting fame as the action had at the time should have pleased the Women's Christian Temperance Union. It was reported as a triumph by sober American infantrymen over a frenzied and liquor-crazed force of Japanese whose officers dressed in their parade uniforms and charged, Samurai swords in hand, directly upon the American defenses.

One minor episode in the mop-up of the island did have this forlorn nature—a death grapple of Drys vs. Wets. But it was the only liquefacient angle of an otherwise arid campaign. To that boozy bit of battle, which came to be known as the Fight on Saki Night, these notes relate.

By the third night of operations, the main forces of the Japanese had already been defeated and put to flight. Makin, which is also called Butaritari, is a greatly attenuated island, being about eleven miles long, with an average width of three hundred yards. The center of enemy resistance was a strongly fortified zone slightly more than one mile in length which was covered at each end by a shore-to-shore tank trap with supporting entrenchments and pillboxes. From barrier to barrier, this zone was studded with deep log-walled shelters, trenches and machine-gun posts, these works being so stoutly constructed that field artillery hardly dented them. The beach flanks were also covered by fire trenches.

Our operations on the first day smashed the West Tank Barrier, the First and Third Battalions of the 165th Infantry Regiment advancing directly toward it after landing on the western beaches while the Second Battalion stormed it from behind after landing on the north shore. Within two hours thereafter, the beachhead was extended to the south shore. The enemy garrison was thereby split in two, and those Japanese who had been driven to ground in the area of the West Tank Trap by our preliminary naval gunfire were destroyed during the first afternoon.

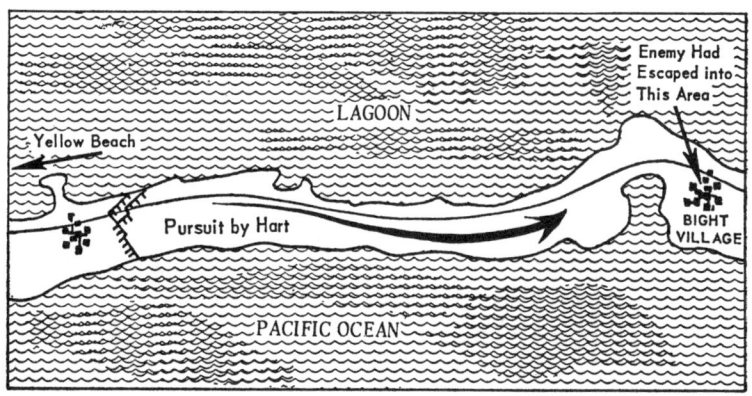

Advance by Hart's Battalion

On the second day the Second Battalion advanced only 800 yards toward the East Tank Trap, its progress being slowed by a network of enemy works extending the entire distance. Artillery fire by the supporting medium tanks, even when directed from 25-yard range, affected the Jap shelters hardly at all. The enemy soldiers remained within the blast-proof entrance; their majority would neither fight back nor surrender. Infantry small arms had no effect on them. They had to be blasted apart by 25-pound charges of TNT tossed through the baffle doors. Tree and ground snipers were plentiful in the area and the dense tropical vegetation combined with the ubiquity of the native *bobai* (taro) pits— an almost infallible trap for tanks—slowed men and armor to a snail's pace. After struggling all day, Second Battalion was still 300 yards short of the barrier when sunset came.

Undetected, at some time around midnight, the Japanese manning the works on our immediate front pulled stakes and slipped away, retiring eastward. The Third Battalion passed through the Second soon after dawn and attacked. But its bullets and the artillery concentration which preceded the rush landed in air. The Third walked through the barrier without having one shot returned. It advanced that day three and one-half miles through the tropical bush, its skirmish line stretching from shore to shore, without a single man coming under sniper fire. These efforts, in the equatorial heat, not only exhausted the men physically but gave them a false feeling of security. Gilbertese who had seen the Japanese retiring eastward by night said that not more than forty-five or fifty remained.

Just before dark, halt was called, and Third Battalion went into defensive perimeter. Had time remained in which to reconnoiter the immediate front, it still would not have been done. Men were too tired. It could be read in the sagging knees, the lack-luster eyes, the drooping jaws, the slavering lips. Officers did not bother to inspect the frontal guns to make sure that bands of fire were interlocking. They were too tired. They watched listlessly while the weapons men went through their motions. Most of the soldiers had dropped their packs and entrenching tools in the morning when they thought they were bounding into a fire fight. Now that they needed them, the lack of tools made little difference. Many a man said it: "I'd rather die than dig; I'm too goddam tired." Even good soldiers get that way when pushed too far. A few of them tried to scoop out shallow foxholes with their gloved hands but the interlaced roots of the forest made it impossible. Some pulled coconut logs parallel to one another and lay down between them for protection. Others sprawled in the open, careful only to prop sticks under the small canopy of netting so that it would ride away from the face, more worried about the mosquitoes than the Japanese. The few who carried K-ration packs didn't bother to open them; it wasn't worth the effort.

In this way Third Battalion came to its sorrowful bivouac, still capable of playing a monstrous joke on itself while being too pooped to laugh at it. The companies had advanced nearly four miles through enemy ground without hearing a bullet crack or sighting one hostile. Then by sheer chance, they halted and made ready for the night within forty-five yards of a well-prepared enemy position fully hidden by the dense vegetation. Had a two-man patrol gone that far forward while the twilight held, the enemy position would certainly have been uncovered.

At a machine-gun post midway of the perimeter front, Corporal William Lilly almost made it. He prowled twenty-five yards to the front of his gun just to look things over, and might have gone farther. It wasn't that he suspected the ground, but because he was hunting for a souvenir. There were two thatch huts amid the bush. In the first one he found a grass (hula type) skirt and so he didn't go on to the second hut. He hung the skirt on a palm tree to dry, intending to send it to his girl in Brooklyn. Later in the night the skirt helped save his position. So we need behold Corporal Lilly with mixed feelings. He was stronger than most of the others, or he would not have moved at all. But moving, he employed his strength to walk away from his gun and chase after a skirt in the jungle.

The left flank of the perimeter hugged the lagoon and the right embraced the ocean shore, the front measuring about 300 yards with Company I on the left and K on the right. Heavy weapons of M were the pivots of this eastward-facing line and around them most of the night's action ed-

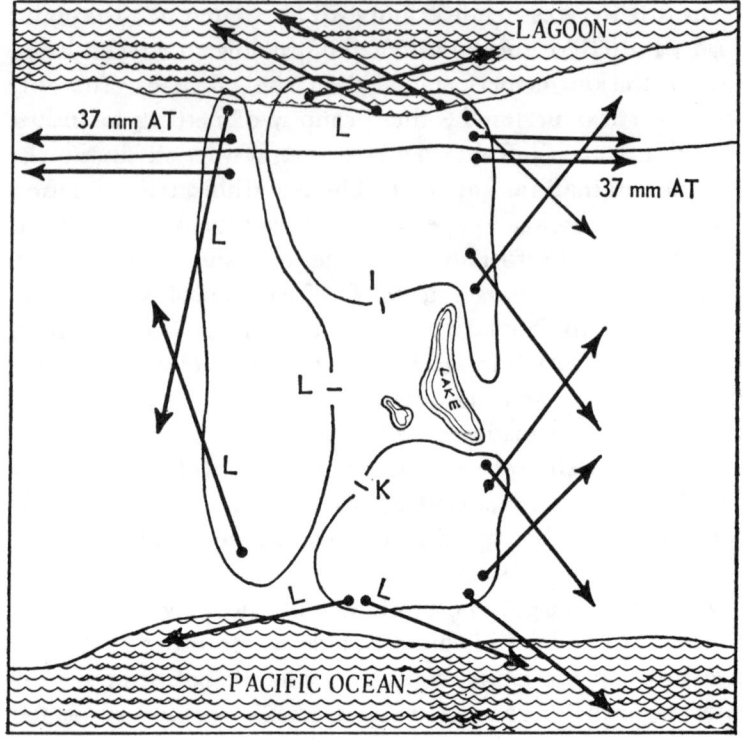

Hart's Perimeter Defense

died. L covered the rear, and except for loss of sleep and an occasional grenade was little disturbed.

On the left flank the main dirt road of Butaritari Island ran parallel to the lagoon within twenty-five yards of the shore. The two antitank guns were placed on either side of it. At 1900 the riflemen covering this position saw something moving toward them through the dusk but held their fire when they heard a child crying. About twenty-five or thirty Gilbertese were then permitted to advance to within our lines. The darkness had thickened until it was almost impossible to see forms and faces; it was learned later that the Japanese had driven these people forward;

it was believed later that aided by this screen and mingling with the Gilbertese, the first handful of snipers infiltrated inside the perimeter.

Ten minutes later another group was heard coming down the road. Another baby was heard crying. A detachment of the Engineers to the left of the road didn't trust the sound of that baby's voice and opened fire with a machine gun. Those were the first shots fired by our side. They scattered the advancing Japanese and from that moment on the action was continouous.

Corporal Louis Lula at the AT gun on the right side of the road had watched Japanese running back and forth across the road trying to draw the American fire. Other Japs crawled forward through the underbrush to within twenty yards of the gun. The crew could hear them as the branches crackled. Occasionally they would yell, "Heil Hitler!" or "Blood for the Emperor!" or call Americans by name. Lilly kept his men down and held his fire.

But there was hellapoppin around the other gun where Sergeant Edward Pasdertz occupied the left of three foxholes containing his nine men. Private First Class George Graham had lobbed a grenade into three Japs trotting along the road toward the gun. They scattered. One charged into Pasdertz's trench, was shot from six feet, and reeled away in the dark to drop into the foxhole at the right. As he fell, a Jap grenade landed by the foxhole. Under the double impact, the three men in the foxhole scrambled out and ran toward Pasdertz. He thought they were Japs and was ready to bayonet the lead man, then held his weapon an extra split second to make sure. A choked voice said, "Don't! It's Mac!" and Pasdertz lowered his gun. The three men crowded in. A groan was heard from the right flank; Pasdertz wasn't sure whether the Jap was alive or one of his own men had been wounded. "Feel his feet," he told Corporal George Ammiano. "If they're bare, shoot him." Ammiano crawled over toward the groaner, felt his feet, found them bare, shot.

A second Jap ran obliquely past the front of the gun. Private First Class Frank Jankowski stood in his foxhole, fired five rounds and brought him down. The third Jap, having gotten inside the perimeter, came running forward and kicked Corporal William Vernetti in the head with his bare feet as Vernetti sat up in his foxhole. Pasdertz looked up to see a man rushing him in the darkness, bayonet forward. Not wishing to make another mistake, he yelled, "Who are you?" The Jap leaped clear over him and ran for the beach. Pasdertz jumped up and fired his remaining shots at 20- to 25-foot range. He saw the Jap's shoulder jerk high and then go down against the skyline.

Pasdertz had sent one of the three extra men back to his own foxhole. Before he could send the second one, he heard a thump, yelled "Grenade!" and flattened himself. The grenade exploded, the explosion momentarily illuminated the position, and six Japs charged in with bayonets before the gun crew could get up. In his foxhole on the right, Private Randolph Slatner stood up, firing his BAR from the hip; the machine gun to the left of the AT gun opened fire. The six bayonets went down.

When the grenade went off, Vernetti had felt a terrific jar on his left side, and then something warm trickled down his leg. He thought his hip had been blown open, felt it, found that his canteen had been ripped apart and his leg was running water; a second later he discovered that the fragments had ripped open his face and he was bleeding from several wounds. McAllister held up his hand; Pasdertz found it sticky with blood from a wound above the elbow. He told Jankowski to cover the front. Then he gave the wounded men sulfa tablets and began putting a tourniquet on McAllister.

At that moment Lula's gun on the right side of the road opened fire. Lula had not been able to see any of the action around the left gun, less than twenty yards away, and could provide no help. His first glimpse of the enemy was this:

He saw twenty Japs at twenty-five paces marching down the clearing on the right side of the road, column of twos, keeping step, their pieces at right shoulder. The front files were carrying a machine gun. Lula heaved a grenade and jumped for his AT gun. A Jap grenade thumped into the American position and Lula kicked it aside. The Japs made a convulsive move leftward as the grenade dropped in the road, but were still a solid body, grouped around their machine gun. From off to Lula's right, Private First Class George Porter threw a grenade with a shout of "That for Tojo, you sons of bitches!" (Porter does not remember saying anything. The other crew members recall it clearly and he says it must be so.) The grenade hit the foremost Jap in the chest, dropped to the ground, exploded. Just in time. Lula had reached the AT gun, closed the breech and fired. He had no need to aim because it was dead on the target and canister loaded. As the enemy files reeled and fell Private First Class Edwin Love, ten feet to Lula's right, emptied his carbine at the mass, loaded, and emptied it again. Seventeen enemy dead were found there in a heap the next morning, piled around their machine gun, ten feet in front of Lula and his gun. After that execution, the corporal stayed at his gun for a while. He found it good work, he said, and preferred to do it by himself.

The continued fire on the right, and silence on the left, gave Pasdertz misgivings about why his second AT gun (a comforting euphemism, the weapon being a 37-mm) had taken no share in the action. He left Jankowski with the wounded and crawled to it. The man on the gun was in a state of nervous collapse and unable to answer questions. So Pasdertz put Corporal Alton Pierce on the gun, told him to fire a few rounds of canister and then return to the foxhole, as the gun position was badly exposed. In the foxhole on the left, Vernetti, the wounded man, heard the gun start up, then grow silent again, became convinced that the Japs had taken it, grabbed his rifle and started crawling up to recapture it. Jankowski grabbed him and convinced him that Pasdertz still had command of the gun.

The pressure slackened. All around the perimeter as the fire fell off, the Japanese began beating their prayer sticks with the monotonous cadence of jungle drums. In the bush immediate to our front, a few Japs crawled forward to retrieve their wounded or to work their rifle bolts noisily in order to draw down fire and spot the position of our riflemen. Periodically there was throaty singing and laughter from the palm forest ahead, and when a silence held momentarily, our men could hear a gurgle as of liquor being drunk with great gusto. Some of the Japanese who had been mangled by canister, losing a hand or a foot, dragged themselves back to shelter, loaded up on saki, then crawled off into the bush to bleed to death. There were shouts for Hitler, shouts for Tojo. In between salvos of knee-mortar fire, a voice from the enemy lines kept shouting: "Come on in, you Yankee bastards, and we will treat you right." The Jap snipers who had infiltrated our left flank (twenty were found dead inside our lines the next morning) kept up an intermittent fire from the ground and trees between the AT gun and the machine gun on the lagoon side, harassing the gun crews of these weapons.

On the extreme left of our line, a Jap officer loomed above a foxhole in which lay Private First Class Elio Bizzari. Yelling, "I've got you, Joe!" the Jap lunged forward; his sword ran Bizzari through, entering just above the heart but missing the vital organs. Private Gerard L. Heck, occupying the shell hole with Bizzari, shot the Jap with his carbine but didn't finish him. Bizzari pulled the sword out of himself, drew his trench knife, leaped on the Jap and made it a good job.

During more than an hour in which the enemy pressed the attack with knee mortars and sniper fire, our men countered only with grenades. Then Pasdertz heard a crackling of leaves and dead palm fronds as if a number of men were crawling toward the gun. He and Pierce got there first and fanned the foreground with canister. Before they could fire three rounds, Pasdertz's rifle was smashed by his side and a second bullet, from the rear, hit the breech ring next to Pierce. Pasdertz then crawled back to the foxholes and divided his men, half covering the front and half the rear. His greatest trouble at this time was that despite the enemy fire, which knocked out another rifle and one more carbine, the exhausted men dozed. So he kept making the rounds, pushing grenades into their hands and telling them to throw. There was need of it. Twice again groups of Japs charged in at a run. They were stopped by Slatner with his BAR and by the machine gun on the left. Not long before dawn, another enemy machine gun opened fire from thirty yards, directly in front of the left AT gun. Ammiano crawled off to the right a couple of lengths and fired with his carbine to draw the enemy fire away from the AT gun. Then Pierce crawled forward and gave them some canister, hitting the gun with his last round of ammunition. At the right gun, Lula also exhausted his canister supply in spraying the enemy front. The machine gun in our center (Schwartz's gun) was under heavy fire and Lula traversed the AT gun over that way to try to help Schwartz. His first round of high explosive set fire to a stump within the enemy lines, which would have helped if his second round hadn't blown the fire out. He continued shelling the woods until only two rounds were left at the gun. By that time, the BAR and all of the carbines at the right-hand gun had jammed and an M1 had been hit and ruined by a Jap bullet. There were only two carbine clips, one grenade and two cans of BAR ammunition left in the antitank position.

The Fight on Saki Night II

At the machine-gun position on the right flank, next to the ocean, the early part of the evening had passed quietly. The men heard the firing on the left but there was no pressure on their immediate position. At about 2310, Private First Class George Antolak saw three shadows moving in from seaward, two crossing his front, one slipping past his right flank; they were within four steps of his foxhole when he first felt their presence. His rifle was half on safety; excited, he threw it all the way on, instead of off, and then tried to pull the trigger. There was no chance for a second try. He jumped up and even as he dove forward threw his rifle at the Jap's face. It spun the Jap off balance, and saber in hand, he fell into the foxhole. Antolak fell on top of him, wedging the saber against the Jap's chest. Underneath the two struggling men was Corporal Charles Steadman, pinned for the moment by their weight. Private First Class Carl Samuels, who had just been relieved by Antolak, took his helmet off and began beating the Jap over the head, hitting with the edge. He released his hold on Antolak, who broke loose, grabbed the saber, and ran the Jap through. Antolak then returned to his gun and fired about fifty rounds in the direction where he'd last seen the other two Japs. Then they all relaxed; Samuels sat on a corner of the foxhole and waited with his carbine. Fifteen minutes passed, and the second Jap came on at a slow run. When Samuels saw him, he was "too close to shoot." Steadman, who was behind Samuels, fired just as the Jap also fired, from the hip. It sounded like one report. Steadman got the Jap bullet in his right hand and the Jap, hit in the shoulder, tumbled into the foxhole. Samuels hit him in the head with the barrel of his rifle, then swung on him with the stock, which fell apart at the first blow. Steadman put the muzzle of his piece against the Jap's head and pulled the trigger.

Sergeant Chester Dey, though only five feet away in another foxhole, had taken no part in this episode. He said: "The Japs were doing all the yelling. My men said nothing. So I figured they were doing all the killing." Rather heavy grenade fire had begun to harass this corner of the perimeter and, not knowing that the enemy was pressing a knee-mortar attack all along the front, Dey began to worry that the grenades might be coming from inside the perimeter. He crawled back to make a check. As he reached the first foxhole on his left, Corporal Tom Padia came crawling into it from the other side. They talked for a few minutes. More grenades dropped and Padia was hard hit in the upper arm. Dey tried to patch him up but the wound was too high for a tourniquet. He started crawling back for help and then his own arm went limp; he realized for the first time that he had been hit by the same grenade. He felt blood trickling down his chin and found wounds on his face also. So he crawled to the machine-gun position on his left. The men bandaged him and he remained there until daylight.

The Second Platoon of M was about a hundred yards inland from the lagoon. Its left machine gun was about thirty-five yards south of the road and its second gun, seventy-five yards or so. It was in front of the left of these two guns that Corporal Lilly had gone hunting and found a grass skirt. Somewhat beyond the native hut where he had lifted his souvenir there was a rise of ground; had Lilly continued to this point, he would have found a machine-gun nest and a large air raid shelter established in this ground. The Japanese in falling back from the citadel area had gone directly to this prepared position and were compactly bivouacked there when the Third Battalion halted for the night. Thus the two camps abutted each other. The center machine gun had been sited away from the high ground held by the Japanese, and looked toward 0230 across a large taro patch. What ultimately saved the position was that a group of large trees, coconut palms principally, intervened between the high ground held by the enemy and the American machine gun.

At the gun was Private First Class Louis Zwick. He was covered at the gun position by Private First Class George Carpenter with an M1. There was no room for Corporal Lilly and Private Garren Whitlock and so they lay in the open a little behind the gun, where they were about half exposed to fire from in front. The crew heard the skirmish on their left but held their own fire until 2000 when the enemy began infiltrating toward the gun. Snipers from the far side of the taro patch kept up a harassing fire. Private First Class Carpenter fired six clips with his M1, without seeing any clearly defined targets, and then Zwick opened with the machine gun, firing in bursts of five and six. He could see no one, but Japanese grenade and rifle fire, and occasional bursts from the machine-gun nest on the mound, were agitating the men around him, and Zwick felt he had better do something. So he maintained his fire. At about 2200 he began to worry because he thought his ammunition supply was running low and he crawled rearward to see about a replenishment. A grenade exploded in front of his face and he felt the blood running down his cheeks. He became faint and crawled back to the gun. Fire was resumed. By midnight, Zwick and Carpenter felt too cramped in the arms to continue and they asked Lilly and Whitlock to take over. They then fell back a few feet and tried to rest, Carpenter a little to the fore. Zwick heard a noise in the undergrowth and asked Carpenter to flatten out so he could fire over his head.

"It's only a hog," said Carpenter, and sat up. Then a hand grenade dropped right on them and exploded as it hit. Carpenter and Whitlock were hit and lay still. Zwick thought they were dead. He jumped for the machine gun and opened fire. His first tracer cut through the grass skirt which Corporal Lilly had hung out to dry, and set it ablaze. By its light, Zwick saw three Japanese; the one who had thrown the grenade was fifteen feet away; the others were beyond the grass huts. Zwick shot two of them and Sergeant John McGovern of M, who was in a foxhole slightly to the rear, threw a hand grenade at the third. Zwick put the gun on him, also, and at that moment the gun ceased firing, and he had to put in another box of ammunition.

The first round was a short, and the gun wouldn't feed. Zwick couldn't get it started. He then grabbed his carbine, but in his hurry he jammed that weapon, also, and couldn't free it. He called to Carpenter, Whitlock and Lilly each in turn but got no answer. (Why Lilly didn't answer is not clear. Lilly says only that he can't remember.) Zwick therefore figured that all others at the gun were dead and that he'd better crawl back and report the situation to the Lieutenant. Right after he started, Carpenter regained consciousness and began calling for Private Riney. In a foxhole to the left rear were Private Morris Schwartz, Private James Riney, and Private Herschel Patton. Schwartz, a New York Guardsman for six years, had been busted from corporal a few months before for "inefficiency." The lieutenant who reduced him had said to Schwartz, "Don't take it too hard. Some day you may learn to be a soldier." So spoke Lieutenant Murray, who was still commanding Schwartz.

Trouble had already come to this foxhole. The Japs had repaid in kind when Sergeant McGovern heaved his grenade and the bomb landed between Patton and the edge of the hole. Schwartz and Riney scrambled out. Patton didn't follow. Schwartz, well out of the hole, lunged back for him, grabbed his shoulders, and pulled him along. They were

Enemy Bunker Next Hart's Position

out of the hole when the grenade exploded, but a piece of metal hit Patton in the neck, killing him. Schwartz and Riney dropped into a ditch farther to the rear. A few minutes later they overheard Zwick report the situation to the platoon commander. Said Schwartz to Riney: "If they're all dead up there and the gun's out, let's go!" They crawled forward. Schwartz checked the three men right away and found that Lilly was sound and the other two only wounded. He asked Lilly about the situation but Lilly wouldn't talk; he was afraid that even whispers carried to the Jap lines. He said: "Boy, am I glad to see you two!" and relapsed into silence. But he kept firing the M1 while Schwartz worked on the machine gun. In the interval, there came a yell from the rear; McGovern had been grenaded and he was shouting for a first-aid man: "Christ, O'Keefe, they got me, they got me. You got me, you Jap sons of bitches, but I'll be back." Schwartz kept working on the gun. The weirdest touch in all this weird scene—from the grass hut a chime clock sounded the hour; until dawn came, waiting for the clock to strike was more unnerving to the American crew than was the enemy fire. The wounded were crowded so close around the gun that there was no room for Riney. So Schwartz sent him back to the foxhole. In five minutes, the gun was going again.

Schwartz figured that Zwick had been giving his position away; he decided to fire never more than two rounds at a time. He did no firing unless he heard a sound or thought he detected movement in the dark. When he heard talking in the bush ahead, he fired in the direction of the voices; when the fire was returned, it made a slight flash and he made that his target. He felt, rather than heard, something in the underbrush, and he said to Lilly: "Bill, I think they're coming up." They peered into the darkness but could see nothing. Then Lilly saw a roundish object rising above and obscuring the silhouette of the hut and realized that it was the head of a man, close to him. Only then he heard the man muttering to himself. He fired at six-foot range and the impact was so great that the man tumbled halfway back to the hut.

Just before dawn the oil and patches in the spare-parts kit in front of the position burst into flames and lit up the area. Rifle and machine-gun fire then rained on it from the Jap lines and the men had to lie flat; it was 0615 before they could move. Corporal Robert O'Keefe of the 165th Medical Detachment, having been turned back twice by enemy fire, got up to the position on his third try. He put his hands under Carpenter's back to move him slightly; a Jap bullet went between his arms and hit Carpenter in the body. Lieutenant Joseph Cason of M then made his move. He had been fairly busy through the night; he had heard Schwartz take the gun over and had figured it was safe for the time being. Now, with the coming of light, he was afraid that the Japs might try to rush it. So he sprinted for the rear, betting his speed against the chance that one of our own men would mistake him for a Jap and plug him. In a few minutes he returned with a rifle platoon and three light tanks to relieve Private

Schwartz, who was then spraying the trees ahead. It was full daylight and he wanted to clean out the snipers before giving over. Twenty-three Jap dead were counted in front of Schwartz's machine gun. We all believed that an additional ten to fifteen had been either killed or desperately wounded at the spot and pulled back into the bush by their comrades. The Japanese on Makin seemed at all times concerned to conceal their losses. They hid their dead in the woods; they dug holes and buried their weapons like dogs burying old bones and toward the end a few of them appeared weaponless.

The sides of the perimeter saw little action; the rear, practically none. But in that area next where the tanks were bivouacked, the night had its touch of comic relief. Private First Class Patrick Howard and Private First Class James Ricker shared a foxhole somewhat more than a hundred yards to the westward of the front line. They had dug the hole together but it wasn't very deep. The mosquitoes bothered them and after they had talked for a while, Howard brought a mosquito bar from the jeep and pulled it down over his head, holding it with both hands from the inside. A grenade showered the hole with dirt and the mosquito bar came off. Howard looked toward the ocean and whispered to Ricker: "Do you see what I see?" Whispered Ricker: "I do." It was then too late to reach for the BAR's; the black shape moving close to earth had almost reached them. At five feet it suddenly reared to full height. In one bound, Howard was out of his foxhole and casting his mosquito bar over the head of the Japanese. As he made the cast, something whistled above his head and stirred his shirt sleeve in passing. Ricker, who hadn't moved, had seen the Samurai sword rise above Howard's head and then cleave the air as the Jap struggled with the mosquito bar. Then both figures vanished into darkness, the Jap running for the ocean shore and Howard for the jeep. This encounter ended in a perfect draw. Howard had picked up his BAR in the getaway, intending to spray the Jap from the cover of the jeep. When he got there, he found he had left the clip behind. There were other small individual skirmishes around and inside the perimeter. Others in the foxholes received grenade and mortar fire, became wounded, or remained clear and answered with grenade and rifle. Others found themselves engaged at close quarters by Jap snipers. The weight of the attack fell, however, on those portions of the perimeter which have been described in these notes and the repulse was the work of a relatively few infantrymen who were able to think clearly and courageously when the pressure was on. Those who were only slightly to the rear of them were in the position of uneasy onlookers, bound by the character of the defense to take little part in the action. The notes are therefore some measurement of the capacity of the average American infantryman for making a proper decision in an altogether unusual situation. Throughout the engagement, the Doughboys who kept the perimeter unbroken without losing a weapon to the Japanese, served virtually as isolated outposts and the arms they bore, especially the grenade, served them very well.

THE AFFAIR AT THE PIGPEN

Shirtless on Kwajalein

ONE passage is missing from this story. The censors struck it when the story was first published in wartime, thinking it too cruel. There is a reference to the incident in my *Men Against Fire*. In deference to the censors' judgment, the name of the victim will be left unmentioned.

In his worst moment during the Burton Island fight, with his platoon stuck tight, Lieutenant Blue crawled forward to the boy hugging ground at the apex of the sprawled formation. He whispered: "Get up and move." The kid answered: "You know I can't do that, Lieutenant; nobody can live in that fire." Blue said: "I say get up and go!" The kid screamed: "OK, Lieutenant. So the whole goddamned United States wants to kill me, does it? Well, watch me die!" He sprang forward. While he was in midair, a bullet cluster got him in the head and splattered his brains.

War for the infantryman is a very personal affair. Every detail of the fight around the pigpen underscores that rather elementary truth. It was personal for Deini and for Private Howell, the lad who went prowling for the front line, not knowing he was it, and who died before he was given time to understand. In this nuclear age, it is just as personal for the Special Force fighter hunting guerillas in the South Vietnam Delta as it was for any Redcoat under Braddock who learned the hard way that having close company just makes a broader target for Indian arrows. In this particular, war never changes.

The whole Kwajalein campaign was very personal for me in a highly embarrassing way. For the first landing, I was attached to this same Battalion. Hartl's men were my companions on the pleasant ride to the far atoll. The first go with the enemy on Ennylobegan Island on D Day was for them a soft-snap triumph and for me a disaster. Only a handful of Japs were on that spit which partly covered the entrance to the lagoon, and they were quickly dispatched. My anguish came of the fact that the Higgins boat carrying my toilet kit and B-bag crashed on the coral reef at the Ennylobegan landing and went to the bottom.

In jig time, a kindly government paid me $265.20 for what I had lost. But that didn't help a bit while the shooting was on. On campaign, friendship stops short of resupplying a man with what he loses through a coxswain's carelessness. That meant no soap, no razor, no salt pills, no nothing. So I wore throughout the five days what I wore and carried going ashore—infantry boots, short green-twill pants, undershirt, one cartridge belt, carbine, eyeglasses and steel helmet. The rains came. My billet was a foxhole in the sand under an emaciated palm. Fortunately, the nights were not too chill.

The battle over, I reported aboard the U.S.S. *Rocky Mount,* Admiral Kelly Turner's command ship, and said: "I come begging, cap in hand; please let me bathe and then dress me decently." A kindly lieutenant took pity on me. I was outfitted with two complete wardrobes of seagoing khaki and a commander's leaves, which have a bright gleam of their own. Ever since, I have walked aware that I owe the U.S. Navy a great debt. Now that the statute of limitations has run out, let it try to collect.

Colonel Zimmerman, Hartl and all others of the 17th Infantry were officers of unusually high caliber. It was a joy to serve with them. The comradeship and the lasting recollection of such men are the payoff for all the hardship that attends accompanying them to their supreme trials.

The Affair at the Pigpen

THE First Battalion, 17th Infantry, passed the day of 2 February (D plus 2 days) on Ennylobegan Island, cleaning equipment, sunbathing, and hunting for souvenirs. The quest for souvenirs brought grief to two men, one of them a staff sergeant named Deini. In fooling with a Jap pistol, he shot a comrade in the stomach. It seemed as if the man would probably die.

Meanwhile the Battalion commander, Lieutenant Colonel Albert V. Hartl, had received orders: The First Battalion would attack Ebeye Island the next morning. It was certain not to be a snap assignment like Ennylobegan Island. Ebeye, the third island north of Kwajalein on the eastern side of the atoll, held a Jap seaplane base. It was known to be strongly garrisoned. Ebeye's code name was "Burton."

So Hartl thought over the case of Sergeant Deini and figured that, having lost one man, he couldn't afford to lose two. He called Deini and he said to him: "I'm not going to do anything about you. That man may die. In any case, we can't use him this time. That's your fault. You can square it by doing enough fighting for two men." Deini, who was a stevedore on the San Francisco docks in normal times, took it pretty grimly. He said he would do his best.

The mile-long, 250-yard wide target island was battered throughout that day by naval gunfire and air strikes. In the afternoon, Hartl's executive officer, Major Maynard E. Weaver, reconnoitered it first from the deck of a destroyer and then from a naval observation plane. He was over the island for two hours. Most of the buildings seemed to have been leveled by the bombardment, but Weaver noticed that there were heavy concrete structures and fire trenches still in good condition at the north end of the island on the ocean side. Since the landing was to be made at the south end, on the lagoon side, it seemed probable that the American right wing would carry the heaviest burden during the attack.

Hartl's Battalion went ashore at 0930 on 3 February (D plus 3 days) after a preparatory hour-long bombardment by cruisers and destroyers. The Ebeye attack plan called for a balanced distribution of force across the island, with both flanks evenly weighted with arms and personnel. As it worked out, however, the enemy was by no means evenly distributed. Weaver had seen from the air that the heaviest buildings

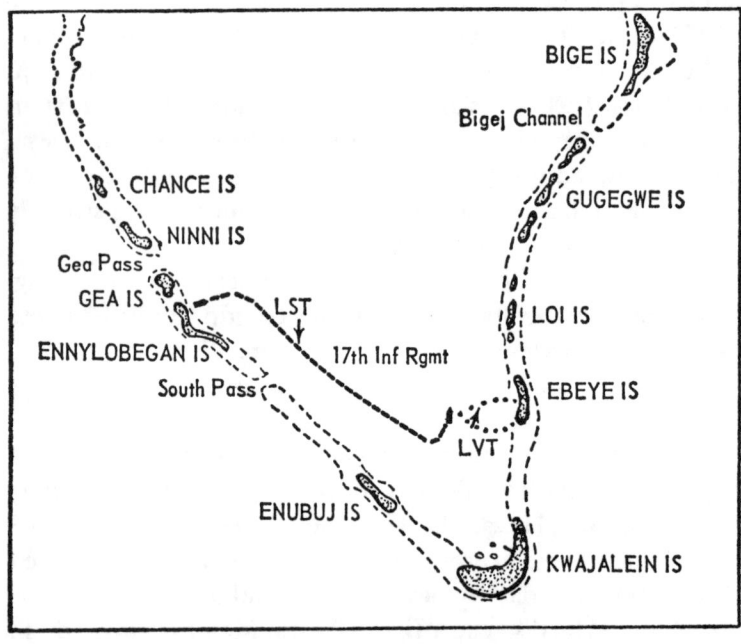

The Kwajalein Group and Lagoon

were on the ocean side of the island, where Company A was to operate.

That seemed significant; on Kwajalein Island, where the fighting was still in progress, the heaviest fighting occurred always where the enemy could make most use of his walls and cellars. But on Ebeye Island there were no pillboxes, fire trenches or underground works of any kind in between the shattered buildings. Thus there was little reason for the Japanese to cling to the built-up area, it having no special strength. It seems probable that a large-scale redistribution of the garrison took place as a result of fire concentrations on the outer side of the island, and that they chose to defend most heavily on the lagoon side because it provided better ground cover. Company C carried the fight on the first day. One platoon did most of the fighting for the company.

The landing was unopposed. The Third Platoon, which was to be in support position for the company during the advance up the island, landed in the first wave with the engineer detachment. It had come ashore in Alligators (a new type of landing boat). Two of them stopped on the reef instead of going to the beach, and the men had to wade ashore through waist-deep water. One man fell into a shell hole and lost his BAR in the water. Private First Class Angelo Ciccotti stepped into another shell hole with the SCR-536 and drowned it out. The platoon pivoted on its left, while the right made the swing around, keeping contact with the platoon from Company A.

LVT's (Landing vehicle, tracked) kept their machine guns going from 300 yards out until they hit the beaches. Buffalos (other small-armored amphibians) blazed away at the foliage line. The scene grew deathly quiet as the line formed and its right swung around the southern tip of the island. It came up even. The line then went ahead a few yards and halted. The Third Platoon had completed its initial task.

The First and Second Platoons, which had followed the

Third in by just a few minutes, halted and took cover at the beach only long enough to get their bearings. Then they came on through the Third Platoon—the First on the right, the Second on the left. For about 100 yards, the line stalked quietly through the underbrush, the men picking their way around uprooted trees and piles of debris.

The Buffalos had gone on up the beach, ahead of the left. Perhaps twenty minutes after the advance had started, they broke the stillness by volleying inland, some distance ahead of the American line. Whether or not this fire did any damage to the enemy, it had one effect on our own forces. It made so much noise that when the first enemy fire crackled above our infantry line, the men did not sense it as a body. There was no sudden, sharp hail of bullets. By squads and by little groups, they heard the warning zing-zing-zing overhead or saw something rip through the foliage above them. This noise was doing them no harm, but by squads and by little groups they flattened as the sounds of danger mounted. It was characteristic action, typical of the manner in which infantry so often loses momentum in attacking through brush-covered country. The faults that produce such stagnation are partly tactical and partly rooted in human nature.

That was true of Company C on this particular day. When the men went to earth, they could not see one another. No man knew where the next man lay on his right and left. To each man came a sense of loneliness. Yet the desire to cling close to the protecting earth was stronger than the desire to move and find one's fellows. It was not instilled in the squad and platoon leaders that their first duty on going to earth was to check the whereabouts of their men so that out of group unity would develop group action. There was no SOP on this point. So they, too, waited until some grew tired of waiting and began calling to their men. Others stayed prone, doing nothing, "waiting for something to happen."

It also is quaintly true of the infantry soldier that his feeling of insecurity rises according to the rate of fire which is coming against him, even when the fire is general and inaccurate. His confidence rises with the lifting or ceasing of the fire. But let him then advance into the area from which the fire has come, and it will require, unless the fire picks up again, all of the driving diligence of his superiors to make him wary and thorough. He can quickly convince himself that all is secure. Many of my infantry studies from the Pacific fighting confirm this point. Company C was to prove it over and over on this day.

A few yards beyond where the center of the line first sensed the fire passing overhead, there was a deep and wide storage bay running toward the lagoon from the left side of the road. It looked like a tank ditch. To the right of the road, some yards on beyond, was a second bay. A large enemy blockhouse and an air-raid shelter were on the far side of it. This was the source of the enemy fire, though our men did not recognize it as such at the time.

The First Platoon was on the right of the road. Some of these men saw the storage bay on the right of the road and figured that if they could get up to it, they would have a good breastwork. But automatic fire lowered and closed in on them and they had to take refuge in a shell crater. The two light machine guns were then brought up and fire was put on the bay. One squad bounded ahead to the bay and fired on the shelter. From the bay it moved off to the right of the shelter, took cover behind some palm stumps, and resumed fire.

The second squad was still some distance back and doing no good there. Sergeant Richard Maples went back to rally it and was hit by a bullet while talking to Lieutenant Isadore I. Feinstein. The squad came on up to the bay. As the men jumped down into it, heavy automatic fire poured in on them from the left rear. They had to hug the back walls of the bay to get away from it, thereby exposing themselves to the fire of the enemy. One gunner had the presence of mind to put his panel on a rifle and wave it high in the air.

The fire stopped. The men believed then that the fire had come from one of our own Buffalos on the lagoon shore.

The company line was already sagging backward, bow-shaped. The First Platoon was moving on the right. Its men were checked periodically by bursts of enemy fire, and the forward movement was sustained through forward rushes by three or four men at a time. There was no real pressure against them, but the circumstances of fire and cover were such that they no longer worked in close cooperation one with the other.

Along the lagoon, a half-squad advancing up the beach had also speeded ahead with no interruption to its progress. This sector of the beach was clear; there were no Japs using the first fringe of cover inshore. So the half-squad went on and outdistanced the men on its right. The other half became echeloned (bent or stepped back) toward the rear as enemy machine-gun fire, coming from the blockhouse on the right of the road, developed against the right flank of the platoon. They went to earth man by man just inside the treeline. It was a fateful pause, for there the Jap artillery found them. Technical Sergeant Walter Feil and Sergeant Carl Swanson were hard hit. The wounded were soon carried out, but the shock of the artillery fire coupled with the effect of the machine-gun fire kept the other men pinned to the ground. They stayed there doing nothing.

These things contributed to the stretching of the line. The center was still well behind, retarded by automatic fire which was ranging across both sides of the road. Technical Sergeant Manford B. Lauderdale, Staff Sergeant John I. Inseth, and Private First Class Clay Vanwinkle, with a BAR, worked up under this fire, trying to get to the left-hand storage bay. They saw three Japs running from the forward shelter—the first enemy soldiers seen by the company.

Sergeant Seth Stear yelled: "There they go. Get 'em, Rip!" But before Vanwinkle could fire the BAR, the Japs ducked

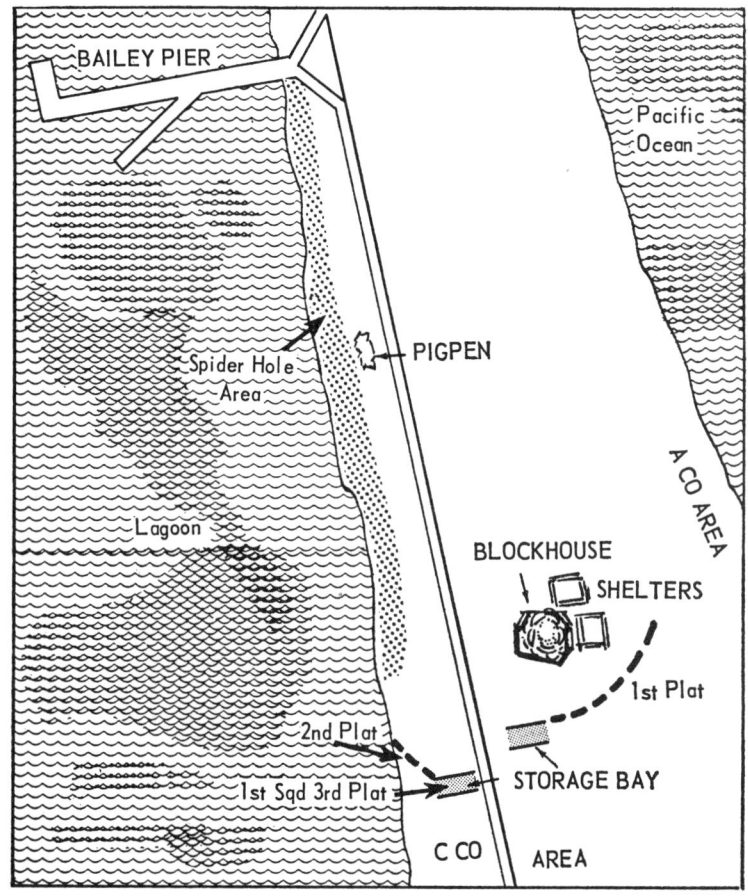

First Phase: Attack Toward the Pigpen

into the bush. The group then threw grenades in their direction.

Over on the far right, Private Percy Johnson, the contact man with Company A, saw four Japs standing in a clearing about seventy-five yards ahead and slightly to the left. He yelled to Lieutenant Erwin Desmonde, his platoon leader: "Come here! I see Japs."

Lieutenant Desmonde looked through his field glasses and

exclaimed: "By God, they *are* Japs!" Desmonde and Johnson fired and so did Private First Class Ballard T. Cogar with his BAR. The four Japs went down—the first men hit by the company.

The reports of contact with the enemy by the First and Second Platoons reached Lieutenant Charles E. Murphy at the company CP within seconds of each other. Lieutenant George E. Linebaugh, who commanded Company C, then took the extra precaution of ordering a Buffalo to advance up the left flank, take station, and stay in readiness to fire at any enemy force coming down the beach. He was worried about the half-squad on the extreme left which was up by itself and in position to be cut off. The Buffalo went forward, stopped thirty-five yards short of the men on the extreme left and began an indiscriminate fire inland which fell among the men who had been checked by the artillery. Sergeant Manuel Mendez yelled: "Cut out that goddam fire!" The Buffalo heard him and drew off.

As the stretching of the line continued because of the advance of the right, men from the center pulled off in that direction and a gap appeared. Sergeant Gilbert Montenegro and his squad moved up automatically into this breach from the support, and, reaching the storage bay to the left of the road, found themselves in the front line. It was a good spot from which to get a clear view of the ground ahead. Montenegro saw that the automatic fire which had been harassing the center came from the blockhouse to the right of the road. The squad stayed there for a few minutes doing nothing about it. Then the tanks came up.

They had been ashore quite a while but did not move up into the action until Linebaugh phoned Murphy to send them along—two tanks on each side of the road so that one pair would arrive in each platoon sector. The pair that came up on the left found the ground difficult and veered to the road. On the right, one tank got stuck in soft ground just short of the front line and the other didn't want to come along until its mate was free. Montenegro went to one of the tanks on the left and told the crew over the hull-attached telephone that he wanted the tank to advance against the shelter to the right of the road.

The tankers replied that they were taking orders only from the Battalion commander. Lieutenant Charles E. Elliott, Jr., got on the telephone and received the same reply. The tanks remained in place while there was hot argument back and forth as to whose authority the tanks were moving under. This added to the heat of a day already made oppressive by large fires which were throwing a choking smoke over the whole area. The tanks then told the Battalion commander that they couldn't proceed because they were being fired upon.

Colonel Hartl replied: "The infantry is even farther forward and is receiving fire." About forty minutes were lost during this futile interlude. Cooperation flagged because the men in the fire fight thought they had the authority to assign targets to the tank crews and the tankers in the absence of clear-cut orders to that effect were trying to duck the hot spots.

During the argument, Privates First Class Gerald D. Draughn and Edward Hodge, who were handling the bazooka, were ordered by Lieutenant Elliott to move up to an advanced position on the right of the road and fire at the shelter beyond the blockhouse. Covered by Private First Class Emmett Mull with a BAR, who came along behind them, they moved sixty yards out in front of the company, having to go that far before the bazooka could bear on the shelter door. Draughn couldn't see his first rocket because the blast blew sand back into his eyes. But he thought it was a dud. The second hit fair on the entrance. He was ready to fire a third when he saw two Japs charging him from the shelter. He yelled: "Get 'em, Hodge!" and Hodge shot one man with his M1. The other had already gone down. Private First Class Jack Winn, from the storage bay, had winged him with a snap shot. The third rocket was fired into the target. By that time the other men of the squad had come up to the two men and they stayed there under cover.

The deadlock between tanks and infantry was ended by a direct order from Battalion. One tank moved forward to attack the blockhouse. It had been told by the Infantry commander to engage with its artillery but it opened the attack with machine guns. The slugs had no effect. At fifty-yard range, the tank then shelled the entrance with its 75-mm gun. The infantry went along with the tank, and with this forward surge, the company line again became fairly straight.

The Second Platoon's First Squad came under automatic fire while moving up the right side of the road toward the blockhouse. Two men were hit. Others in the squad saw Japs taking cover near a burned truck which lay ahead.

Then two more men were hit. These things happened just like that—one, two, three—a matter of split seconds. The survivors figured the fire had come from the Japs hidden around the truck and they grenaded the ground all about it. The fire ceased; the grenades had hit home and that seemed to square things. But what had happened was that a Jap machine gun far over on our left was firing across the front into the American right flank. The half-squad moving along the beach charged and grenaded the machine gun and its crew and could see that it had been working against the men moving up to the blockhouse.

Private First Class Wilbert Jackson had taken cover where he had a good view of the shelter which had been attacked by the bazooka. He saw a Jap rifleman come out of the rear entrance and he shot him with his BAR.

The tank, having blasted the entrance, started on toward the blockhouse. Four Japs rushed it from the doorway as it got even with their position. One threw a grenade at the tracks. It bounced from the tank and the four Japs were cut down by fire from all along the First Platoon's position.

Such were the incidents developing from the first brush

with the enemy, the defeat of his forward positions and the restoration of some mobility to the company. From the rear the 60-mm mortars had barraged the area of the enemy shelters within a few minutes after the line stopped moving. The fire was at 400-yard range, and it was ranging about 200 yards over, on the right of the road. At least one burst was seen by the men in the First Platoon to hit several Japanese crouching in a foxhole. That was the only firing done by the company's light mortars. When the Second Platoon came in check, the men asked Lieutenant Linebaugh to have 81-mm fire put down just ahead of its lines. He refused. He figured that the left was so badly strung out at the time that any fire which could be put down safely would also be ineffective against the enemy immediately engaged.

One BAR man, Private First Class James H. Gatlin, had carried on a one-man mop-up campaign during the first phase of the fighting, working over every debris pile at close range with his weapon. He had been thoughtfully regarding one pile of palm and broken foliage when he saw it move. He fired into it, then lifted the branches and found two dead Japanese, their wounds oozing blood. He then went on, firing into other piles, holding the BAR over sideways so that instead of climbing it went forward, and then turning it over and sweeping back across again. When fired automatically the BAR tends to rise at the muzzle. This is controllable when the firer is shooting prone, but not in firing while standing. Private Gatlin, by turning his BAR half over as he fired it, obtained a horizontal movement of the gun and distribution of his fire along the ground, instead of a vertical distribution. In one other pile he collected three dead Japanese after giving it a burst of fire.

As the platoon continued forward it received a few rounds of sniper fire. When this happened, one or two men began firing at the tops of the few palms that were still standing. This was contagious. More men fired at the tree tops, meanwhile paying little regard to the rubble piles and broken foliage through which they passed. If no fire came from such a spot, they assumed it was safe. It was only when our men began to drop from rifle fire well back of their lines, and the spraying of the tree tops yielded nothing, that they learned to prowl everything they came to, either by dosing it with rifle fire or by tossing a grenade into it. The BAR proved an excellent weapon for this kind of work.

The First Platoon, having freed itself with the aid of the tanks, couldn't understand why the Second Platoon wasn't going ahead. Neither could Company A, which had been moving along easily on the ocean side of the island. The advancing line was supposed to keep roughly straight. The units on the right, although no great distance from the men who had been checked on the lagoon side, were as remote from them in sympathy and in situation as if they had been on another island.

Derisive calls drifted over from the right flank: "You can't win a war sitting on your ass." That galled the men on the left even more than the invidious comparisons made by the battalion staff over the telephone. "If Company A is able to get forward, why can't the left flank of Company C go ahead?" The Second Platoon had no ready answer to any of these critics. Engaged as it was, it had no way of knowing that it was carrying the big load for the Battalion and that the other outfits were comparatively unengaged. The command in the rear couldn't understand this either.

On the other flank, things were going ahead so leisurely that when water in the canteens began to run low, the men had time to cut up the coconuts which littered the ground when the artillery ceased mauling the trees. That flank moved ahead by slow, easy stages to avoid getting too far beyond the Second Platoon's position. Its experiences were in ironic contrast to what had been going on along the left.

The blockhouse by the road was well battered when the tank ceased firing upon it. There were several gaping holes by the doorway, through which a dead Jap lay sprawled.

One of the men from First Platoon tossed a couple of grenades inside and then the line passed on. Before the support got up to it, Staff Sergeant Otis Lasswell, Jr., saw a man from Company D shoot a second Jap as he stuck his head out the door. This made Lasswell wonder if anyone had cleaned out the shelter. He asked Lieutenant Daniel A. Blue if anything had been done to follow up the work of the tank. Blue didn't know. A bulldozer was then brought up to seal the entrance. The driver looked the place over, said: "It's too hot for me," and turned back toward the rear.

Lasswell went after a flame thrower. The flame was shot into all three entrances. The operator then climbed on top of the shelter and shot the flame through a six-inch vent in the roof. "There's no one in there now!" he said to Lasswell when he got down. Lasswell agreed. They started to walk away.

Five Japs came out of the shelter with their hands up. One had been hit by a shell and died shortly afterward. Another had a slight burn on the arm. The other three hadn't been touched.

While they were collecting the Japs, a kitten walked out of the shelter. The troops played with it long enough to discover that it was shell-shocked. When put in any one position, it would stay just that way and blink at them. Lieutenant Desmonde left the men playing with the kitten and trying to stand it on its head. He went on over to the left to see what was holding up the Second Platoon. He wanted to get his own First Platoon forward and he figured that maybe the units on the other end of the line needed a little prodding.

The First Platoon's Second and Third Squads had moved up to the shelter on the right. During the approach, a couple of Japs were seen sitting in the doorway. They ducked back inside. But these enemy soldiers having disappeared, the men took no immediate steps to finish them. They stretched out on the ground around the shelter, resting and waiting for the company's left to get in motion. Half an hour passed.

Private First Class Elmer Powell leaned against one end of the shelter eating a candy bar. At the other end of it, a Jap machine gun fired periodic wild bursts toward Company A. The First Platoon men saw that the Jap was just wasting ammunition so they let him have his fun. On the ocean side of the shelter around the corner from Powell, was another low entryway. A second Jap popped out of it, carrying a machine gun. He stumbled on the steps and the gun went off, alerting the Americans near by.

Private First Class Hjalmar Pederson lay in a shell hole opposite the entrance. Without raising his voice, he said to the man next to him: "My Got, dey're cooming oudt." His second shot crumpled the Jap. Powell dropped his candy bar and leaped for the nearest cover, ten yards off. Private Cogar threw a grenade. It dropped fair into the far opening and exploded right under the Jap who had been shooting toward Company A. There was quiet for a minute or two. Then five distinct explosions were heard inside the shelter.

The men figured that that number of Japs had blown themselves up. In the sudden excitement, their mood changed instantly from extreme carelessness to pronounced caution. They stood at a respectful distance and heaved ten grenades at the doorway. Then they improvised a satchel charge by wiring six blocks of TNT together with a detonator and tossed it in the door. It exploded with a loud report and blew dirt and timber from the building. Right after that the platoon advanced to a position beyond the shelter. Sergeant Romaine Kitcheon, spotter for the mortars, took up a post behind some sand-filled oil drums which protected the entrance to the shelter. He heard a noise, looked up, saw a Jap emerging and shot him through the head.

As the day wore on past noon, the battle lost its sweat for the men of First Platoon. The fires still blazed about the island but a strong wind from the east was whipping the smoke to the lagoon side. The men saw no sign of the enemy. They were through shooting for the day. They idled behind the palm stumps and in small shell craters, and if they snoozed now and then in the strong sunlight, the enemy took no action to rouse them from their slumber. They knew that the left must be having some trouble because they could hear the rattle of automatic fire and the snort of grenades exploding on that flank. But that was someone else's fight, and the sounds signified little more to them than did the distant rumble of artillery breaking over Kwajalein Island, where the battle of the 32nd and 184th Infantry Regiments was wearing into its third day. That 100 yards of mangled palm forest which separated the two platoons made all the difference and their imaginations could not bridge the distance. It was as well so. They could do nothing to help the Second Platoon, and rest is good for weary feet wherever it is to be had. They marked time and they enjoyed the afternoon.

A stray chicken wandered into the First Platoon area. Three of the men ran it down. Then came a pig—a 150-pound pig, one of the farm boys present estimated. The pig seemed unconcerned but was straying back from somewhere up in the battle area. Lieutenant Feinstein had found a grass rope among some Jap stores and was carrying it around for a souvenir. He suggested to Kitcheon that they capture the pig in lieu of anything better to capture. "And I will tie it by the neck," Feinstein said.

"It won't work," said Kitcheon. "You can't hold pigs that way." But he and Private First Class Raymond Cochran ran the pig down. Cochran caught it by the hind leg. The pig squealed and dragged him along the ground and everyone yelled. He and Kitcheon then roped it around the hind legs. In a few minutes it broke away and ran grunting toward the rear. The men kidded Kitcheon. They wondered where the pig had come from. The men of the Second Platoon could have told them.

While the Second Platoon had stayed pinned to the ground in the hour-long lapse which followed its buffeting by the artillery, two medium tanks stood steady in the ground occupied by the support squad. They took no part in the action. The platoon leader tried to talk with the crews. But they didn't respond to the telephone and they wouldn't open up when he hammered on the armor. The foot soldiers saw all this and their reaction was characteristic.

The records of the Central Pacific operation show consistently that whenever tanks and infantry were supposed to be working in close combination and the tanks didn't move, the infantry was always reluctant to go forward. The presence of immobilized tanks is a discouragement. They can stall the movement of an infantry line that otherwise might be quite willing to advance. The Second Platoon got hung up on this rock. Motion was at last restored when on direct order from Colonel Hartl over the radio, the tanks came on up into the ground held by the assault line.

The scattered groups of the platoon responded immediately, and without orders. As the tanks came through, they got up from their cover and moved toward the enemy, even though a wild, harassing fire from rifles and automatic weapons continued to break over the front. Twenty-five yards farther along one tank threw a track on a coconut log and went out of the action. The other tank kept going. It stayed buttoned up and there was no communication. The tank would lurch forward fifteen or twenty yards, the infantry going along with it or a little behind it. Then the tank would stop; the crew wanted to be sure that the infantry was still with them. The infantry would flow on around the sides of it. When the tank again saw the infantry on ahead, it would come through and take the lead for another score of yards.

It was a crazy, jerky advance, continued like a game of leapfrog. But it was appropriate to the situation. For the moment, both arms needed the assurance which came from the presence of the other. As for the infantry movement, some of the men moved ahead at a walking gait with weapons at high port and others moved from cover to cover by short rushes. They advanced, not on orders, but according to their own initiative. If the first man in a group spurted for cover, the others in the group did the same. If two or three in another group started walking out, the whole group moved out the same way. Gradually the rest of the line moved up abreast of the half-squad which had held the advanced position on the beach.

They had advanced perhaps 120 yards when the squad moving just within the line of cover along the shoulder of the beach saw a Japanese caliber .50 air-cooled gun off to its left about twenty feet. The gun was pointed in the direction of the morning landings and is thought to be the weapon which hit three men in the Headquarters group when they came in on a later wave. The tank had passed on beyond the gun after firing a machine-gun burst down into the pit.

Sergeant Roger Horning crawled to within ten feet of the gun and fired one round from his M1 into the magazine. The gun blew up. Some of his men covered him as he crawled on to the pit and looked in. He was face to face with a live Jap who blinked at him; they were so close that they could have bumped heads. It "scared the living hell" out of Horning. He flopped back into a shell hole just at the edge of the pit, a grenade in his right hand and a rifle in his left. As he recoiled, he threw the grenade. It came right back at him, rolling down the sand and settling at his feet.

He looked at it and kept on looking at it; he didn't think either of touching it or of moving away from it. His thought and his body were paralyzed. The grenade was a dud. Seconds passed and he realized that the grenade wasn't going to explode. He jumped up and ran back to the squad, yelling for grenades. There were none at hand. He ran farther back, yelling for a flame thrower. Someone signaled him that the flame thrower was out of order.

Returning to the pit, he found that Sergeant Robert Genung had come up with an improvised satchel charge. Horning threw it at the pit, but he was excited and the cast was wild. The charge exploded across the surface, blowing up dirt all around. The two BAR men who had been covering Horning walked up to the pit, firing as they went. As they reached the edge, one BAR ran out of ammunition and the other jammed. They scurried back to make the necessary readjustments.

"This time," said Horning, "one of you fire during the advance and the other hold fire until you reach the pit." That was what they did. As they pumped lead into the pit, they saw one Japanese fall but they could not see whether anyone was beyond him.

The spider holes began just beyond this gun position. The beach proper, which had been unoccupied during the first stage of the advance, had been organized from this point on with small pits just large enough to hold one man and in such juxtaposition to holes on beyond it that the occupant could move in either direction to quick cover. The holes had been covered with tin sheeting, palm fronds or other camouflage material, and could not be seen from a 10-foot distance. Amid these nests of small and rude individual positions were a number of redoubts built solidly of logs and bulwarked with oil drums or iron sheeting, so that along the beach the enemy ground was much like a crude trench system organized in depth. Flanking the lagoon, railroad iron had been cabled to the coconut trees to repel tanks or other vehicles coming ashore. The Second Platoon was approaching the area generally from the flank, but the detailed defenses of the ground were such that there was menace in every direction.

As Horning crawled on beyond the flank of the machine-gun pit, he saw a layer of palm fronds on the ground twenty yards to the fore. Quite suddenly the palms moved, as if from pressure below, and he knew there was a Jap there. He told Lieutenant Elliott what he had seen, and Elliott ordered him to go forward and prowl the spot.

He crawled on, five, six yards; then he yelled back to Elliott: "I won't go on until I'm sure there's no one in that pit." Elliott threw three grenades in the pit. Horning heard them explode and he crawled on. He got up to the fronds and under the edges he saw a black pit and something moving within. He pulled the pins of two grenades and rolled them over the edge. Both exploded. The Jap inside the hole took death sitting down.

Private First Class Robert Everett had crawled up to Horning while he was working. He then crawled on around the hole. Horning, preoccupied with the grenades, didn't see Everett rise up and stand with his back to another patch of fronds just beyond the first hole. When his gaze rose, there was just time to yell: "Watch it!" A Jap from out of the second hole was making a flying tackle at Everett's knees. Everett spun out of reach, and as he twisted, he jammed the muzzle of his BAR against the Jap's head and pulled the trigger. They went down together, but only Everett got up.

That was the way it went. The holes were everywhere. Each one had to be searched from close up. Every spot where a man might be hiding had to be stabbed out. So greatly was the beach littered with broken foliage that it was like looking through a haystack for a few poisoned needles.

Before the First and Third Squads finished this kind of duty, two men had been killed and eight wounded by fire from the spider holes. The attention of all hands had to be focused on the foreground. The fire which cut the men down came from the spider holes farther up the line. It was the kind of bitter going that made it necessary for the junior leaders to prod their men constantly. The leader of the Third Squad had been trying to get his men forward against the fire. Private First Class John Treager got up, rushed forward about ten yards, hit the dirt, fired a few shots with his BAR and crumpled with a bullet in his head.

Somewhat farther along, a bayonet was seen sticking out through a patch of fronds. The Japanese crouched within it hadn't room to draw in the whole length of the weapon.

Private First Class Edward Fiske fired his BAR at the hole and the dried fronds caught fire from the tracers. At that point Fiske ran out of ammunition.

Private First Class Julian Guterrez then took up the fire with his M1. He stood directly above the hole and fired down into it. Then the hole exploded; the Japanese inside had turned a grenade on himself. A man's shattered arm came flying out of the hole and hit Guterrez on the shoulder, splattering blood all over his face and clothing. The arm bounced off and fell to the side. As Guterrez looked at it, fascinated and horror-stricken, he saw another bayonet rising out of a patch of fronds just beyond the outstretched and still-quivering fingers. He yelled to Private Joe Buchanan behind him. Buchanan relayed a grenade and Guterrez pitched it with all of his might into the patch of fronds. It erupted a shower of palm leaves and blood and flesh.

Guterrez reeled over toward the lagoon to cleanse himself of the blood. Before he could reach the water, in sight of the other men, he vomited along the beach. Thirty minutes passed before he could clear his mind and get going again.

By this time Second Platoon, officers and men, had lost all sense of time. They had come along for several hours, clearing the frond coverings from the spider holes with their bayonets, where they did not first blast them after detecting some sign of the enemy. They were dog tired. Their losses had been fairly heavy. Yet oddly enough, most of them thought it was late morning though the day had worn into late afternoon. Lieutenant Linebaugh had given Battalion Headquarters a report on casualties. He then talked to Lieutenant Elliott about a relief. Elliott went around to his men and told them to halt in place until the Third Platoon came through.

Lieutenant Blue told his men to drop packs and gas masks and the Third moved up, two squads on the line. Each squad had two scouts out front, the leading scout moving about fifteen to twenty yards ahead of the platoon and the second splitting the distance back to the line. No tanks went forward with the men; it wasn't the kind of fight in which tanks could do much good. However, the situation was quiet for the moment. When the Third reached the front, the men of the Second were sitting around tight-mouthed. There was no fire.

The platoon advanced at a walk in squad column and kept going. As they passed the Second, Genung said to Blue: "Tell your men that they must watch out for the spider holes. They must search every one of them." Lieutenant Blue then saw for the first time what Second Platoon had been up against. As far as he could see up the beach, there was a checkerboard of the palm-frond patches. He passed the word to them: "Go at every patch with fire first and then with your bayonet." He kept telling them that that was what they must do.

They moved on twenty-five, thirty, forty yards. There was no enemy fire. The men searched the first few lines of holes diligently, ripping the fronds off with their bayonets. They found nothing. Lieutenant Blue noticed that they had already begun to ease up, hitting a hole and then skipping a hole. They went on another twenty-five yards. The man ahead of Blue stepped across a frond patch and kept on moving.

Blue yelled: "Goddammit, what are you doing—stepping across a hole you're supposed to search? There may be a Jap in there." A Japanese rifle lay across the hole. From underneath, a hand reached up for it before Blue could close the distance. Blue saw the hand; saw, also, that five of his men were beyond it. He took the chance and fired at the hand. The bullet split the hand at the knuckles. The Japanese had started to rise, but Blue's rifle was so close that the blast knocked him back again and the helmet flew from his head. Blue fired two slugs into the back of the Jap's head.

"Start looking into every hole or we'll all be killed!" Blue shouted to his men. It was then that Staff Sergeant Pete

Deini, who had accidentally shot a man on Ennylobegan Island, came to the fight. Deini had been walking along like the others, but had been doing a lot of thinking. He knew there was something wrong with the platoon. He could feel it. He knew the men were afraid. He felt fear in himself. But he wondered how he could feel it in the others. Then he got it. The sergeants had clammed up. The men were accustomed to hearing them bark. When they didn't, the men knew the sergeants were fearful, and they could not rally their own confidence.

He found what to him was the obvious answer: Somebody had to talk it up and keep talking it up; it wasn't enough simply to act or to bark an order after things had gone wrong. He saw his duty and throughout the rest of the afternoon he spark-plugged the whole operation. Moving from group to group, he showed them how the thing had to be done, and he talked as he worked. When he saw men hesitate in front of a spider hole, he went through them, ripped the fronds away, and used the bayonet if the bayonet was needed.

As he worked, he talked without ceasing: "Come on. You can do the same thing. Watch me. There are more of them. Keep busy. Keep moving. Keep your eyes open." Then he moved on to another hole. Deini in person cleared out at least 50 per cent of the positions covered by the platoon and the thoroughness of the other men was due almost wholly to him. The other men acknowledged this. Deini was no great talker. He had an impediment in his speech. But his was the clearest voice sounded by a junior leader during the invasion of Kwajalein Atoll.

Spider holes in large number still confronted the left of the platoon when the right came up to an obstacle of a different kind. Between the road and the shoulder of the beach the ground fell away into a deep swale which had been cleared for about seventy-five feet in both directions. Within the swale was a shelter for pigs. Vines grew all around and over it, and tin sheeting had blown down around the sides so that it was impossible to see clearly what lay within. Forward of this penned area was another small structure—a shed or feed house—lying close to the road.

The left flank, moving along the beach, was about abreast of the pen but had not yet seen it when Private First Class Vern Howell, the front scout of the right-hand squad, came alongside it. He stepped up to the nearest corner and the second scout, Private Clifford Hahn, caught up with him. Howell was puzzled. It was his first time in the lines.

"What is the front line like?" he asked Hahn.

"You're it," said Hahn. "Didn't you know it?"

"Quit kidding me," said Howell.

Replied Hahn: "I'm not; we're the front line right now."

"But what do you do?"

Hahn replied: "You just keep going until you see someone shooting at you. And you keep looking all around."

Howell kept going. The squad had come up even with him and the two scouts continued on, Howell some feet ahead. He paused for a minute and squatted at the forward corner of the enclosure. Then he began to straighten up. As he came half-erect, fire from the pen and the little building riddled him. Then men of the squad saw his body jerk, but he did not fall. He sagged over against the side of the enclosure.

There was no recoil in the platoon. They knew where the fire had come from. They weren't sure whether Howell was dead. But the sight of him standing there motionless and bleeding galvanized them. The squad from the beach moved up to the left side of the enclosure. The right squad pressed up against the rear. They could not lie prone and fire. To bear upon the pen at all, they had to stand erect and shoot down into it. But they gave it everything they had—BAR and rifle fire, grenades and finally satchel charges.

Private First Class Edwin Jeffers, a BAR man, ran up to within reaching distance of where Howell stood, put his

BAR on the hole through which the Jap volley had poured, and kept on firing until he was called back by his platoon leader, who figured that Jeffers would get it just like Howell if he stayed there. The fire was still hot. A first-aid man got up to the men who were firing along the rear of the pen. Howell was pointed out to him. The men figured if Howell could stand he must still be alive.

"Do you think I can get up there?" the aid man asked Sergeant Lasswell.

"That's up to you," Lasswell answered. "I can't tell you to go."

He asked another man and got the same answer.

The aid man, George Johnston, didn't say anything. He took one more glance forward and then ran toward Howell. That was too much for Private First Class Jeffers. He couldn't stand the idea of the man going out alone, and he too went running forward to cover Johnston with his BAR. They reached Howell. The aid man took hold of his shoulder. The figure fell over, and from the manner of the fall, the men of the squad knew he was dead. Jeffers and the aid man tore back for cover.

The fight went on. Lasswell, looking through the rails of the pen saw a wounded Japanese lifting a rifle. He fired three slugs into him. At each hit, the Japanese shook all over but kept crawling toward Lasswell, pulling himself with his elbows. Lasswell gave him four more bullets and the man died. Deini had grenaded the pen from the right and had heard men scream as the grenades went off. He then ran around to the left of the pen. Sergeant Steinkamp saw a Japanese moving toward the rails on the left and killed him with his first bullet. A rifle poked up through the vines in the center. Deini saw it, realized that it was pointed straight at him, ducked instantly.

Private First Class Nick E. Eloff was standing directly behind Deini and the bullet hit him in the wrist. Deini saw that he couldn't get the Japanese marksman from that side, and he whipped back to the right where there was a good opening. He shot the Japanese with his rifle. Then he ran out of ammunition, reached for more and found that a Japanese grenade had cut away his ammunition belt and half of one trouser leg. He had felt the burst but hadn't believed it was that close. He called for a satchel charge, and he heaved it far over the rail at the spot where he had seen the grenade thrower's hand come up from above the timber. There was a terrific explosion which shook down the building inside the pen. Private First Class Thomas Burrescia brought up his flame thrower on the beach side and tried to reach the mass of wreckage with it. But the wind was too strong and the flame blew back on our men.

All of this time Battalion Headquarters was prodding the company commander to get the platoon forward, and he in turn was prodding Lieutenant Blue. He was told to leave the pigpen to Company B which would do the mop-up job, and to get on with the advance. But Blue figured that the commanders were much too remote from his situation to judge of it. Though the pen grew quiet and it appeared that the Japanese detachment which had driven the pigs out of their cover was pretty well liquidated, he still did not wish to leave the guarding of his rear to Company B's hands. He couldn't see the support force and he wanted to be sure.

So the First Squad moved around the pigpen by way of the beach and took position in front of the pen. The support squad came up to the line on the left and the platoon continued forward. A medium tank came along a few minutes later and after the covering squad had moved out of muzzle-blast range, the tank fired three rounds of 75 HE into the pen. Still, a live Japanese was caught crawling from the pen on the following morning.

Spider holes confronted the left of the line for another 150 yards. Deini again led the way through them, working four times as hard as any other and talking to the men all of the time. They reached another Japanese air-raid shelter then.

A medium tank was sent against it. The tank was still pumping .75 shells into it when Company B came through and Lieutenant Blue's men fell back to the mop-up position.

As for the soldier Deini had accidentally wounded by a bullet from a Jap pistol on Ennylobegan Island, the Medical Corps managed to save him to fight in other battles.

WHEN PAPA TOOK PARIS

The Novel and War

FAR from a serious study of battle, "When Papa Took Paris" is a war correspondent's sidebar, written in the name of good clean fun. With few exceptions, the main characters are supernumeraries who merely go along for the ride. War is like that; not even travel is more broadening; one meets the most interesting people. But as with other tourists they do not always see eye to eye.

All my other commentaries in this book have the object of making clear the narrator's place in the landscape, his relation to the forces or his duties as a soldier and observer. Here, none of these is necessary. What I did comes out as the story unfolds.

Aside from that, what needs be said? Perhaps nothing. But I enjoy interposing the personal point of view, and in my work such opportunities are rarely presented. For almost fifty years I have read most of the fiction written of wars in which I have participated. At the end I am more puzzled than at the beginning. What stumps me is the manner in which the critics toss around certain adjectives in praise or damnation, according to their ideas of what war is supposed to be. In this way, because novelists like historians either grow big or starve according to their book sales, there develops a concensus about the nature of man in war which is but vaguely related to human experience. Being neither, I still have not starved.

Now I get to the point. Norman Mailer rose on wings after

writing *The Naked and the Dead*. The critics hailed its realism. Maybe they meant it was hard-boiled, nasty and alien to themselves because the Americans of which they read were like men of another world. But is that "realism"? In the lines in Korea, we had time to ponder; in the final months, it was a slow war. Games had to be improvised. So the question would be asked: "Did you read *The Naked and the Dead*?" There would be a show of hands. The next question was: "Have you ever soldiered with the kind of men you find in that book? Does the story itself seem credible to you?" There would be discussions, but we found no one who held with Mailer. I concede that the exercise was unscientific. The question may have been loaded. The responses could have been prejudiced and badly informed.

After that, I met Mailer at a cocktail hour of the New York Pen Club at which my host was a former General Staff colleague, Colonel Edward Davison, the poet.

Mailer said: "Oh, yes, I know your name. You're the officer who's supposed to get troops to tell the truth of what happened. No one on earth can do that."

I said: "That interests me. What makes you think so?"

Then from Mailer: "Take my last patrol in the Philippines. There were twelve of us. We didn't carry out the mission. It was agreed that we'd tell a certain story to the command. We got away with it. There was no way to make those other eleven men come clean."

I asked, "Why not, Mr. Mailer?"

He said: "Don't you understand? Those other eleven men were Texans."

It was time to walk away. Ted said to him: "Mailer, Marshall is a Texan, from El Paso; that's as far west as they come."

That was the only time I ever talked to Mailer. My turnabout had nothing to do with him as an individual. It was an old story. For years I had known that criticial appreciation of the literature of men in war and my own feeling about it had almost nothing in common. For example, I loved

George Blake's *The Path of Glory*, but it was a complete failure. On the other hand, Theodore Plevier's novels were everywhere praised. I thought they were amateurishly misinformed. Long ago I knew that I could but agree to disagree.

Soon after World War II ended, I picked up a number of *The Saturday Review* which lamented that it had been fought to no avail: not one novel was forthcoming which had the somber realism of Remarque's *All Quiet on the Western Front.* That made everything even. Several years had passed since I did a lecture in Detroit wherein I said that World War I had been fought to no avail because it had produced such a novel as Mr. Remarque's and the critics had insisted on calling it "realistic."

In the intervening period, much water flowed beneath the bridges, more I suspect under mine than under Mr. Remarque's, if one includes Baileys, pontoon bridges and the other temporaries by which an army moves from here to there. But despite all that water, I saw no reason to change my mind.

I criticized Mr. Remarque on two counts—physics and pigs. I said that he wrote in the vein of one suffering from what is now called psychoneurosis but which the British had earlier and more picturesquely described as "having the wind up." I pointed out that he was utterly humorless, though war is often as funny as *Charley's Aunt.* I argued that supreme comedy and highest tragedy must walk hand-in-hand because that is the rule of life just as it is the law of physics that where the light is highest, near at hand will be the deepest shade.

As an illustration, I offered the bit about the pigs. There is an episode in *All Quiet* where two hungry soldiers try to capture a journeyman pig. They have ham and pork chops on their mind. The pig loves liberty and is extremely fast on the getaway. The harder the soldiers try, the more elusive becomes the quarry. He ducks away, just as a hand is about to gather him in. Finally the soldiers bring off a "double pincers envelopment." The pig slips between their legs. And so on and on.

Where I took exception was that, as Remarque described this incident, it was full of the old world pain and of the belly hunger of the poor, starved soldier. Every movement of it was stark tragedy. One caught only the sense of frustration and deprivation, with never an echo of how two human beings were making themselves look like the Katzenjammer Kids in their attempt to liberate a little bacon. In fact, I was relieved when the pig escaped. Two brutes who are so far gone that they can't see the humor in that situation would probably have eaten the poor little devil alive.

Thus, my observations in Detroit years ago, before the coming of an age wherein the elusiveness of pork would become a national issue and our packing-house owners would possess only such hams as they contrived to sit on.

Dwelling at that time only on the theme that war is the stage of divine comedy, as well as of epic tragedy, and that with a few such notable exceptions as *War Bugs* and *The Good Soldier Schweik,* the whole literature of World War I had dismally failed to reflect these fundamental contrasts, I could not possibly foresee that in my own experiences in World War II, one of the most poignant battle episodes would be built around the attempts of soldiers to capture a pig.

That is luck, or coincidence, or call it what you will, possibly Mars playing into my hands so that I could return to Detroit someday with the case proven, or at least the possibility opened that I could stand on even ground with Remarque as an expert on the subject: "Pigs, How to Capture Them in War, Are They or Are They Not Funny."

As already set forth in this book it happened during the Kwajalein Battle, in a fight for an insignificant sand spit going by the code name of Burton Island, which was important to us mainly because the Japs had a small air base there. There being only one official record, I will have to requote from my earlier chapter as to what happened to an American platoon during a slack moment in the engagement:

"A stray chicken wandered into the First Platoon area. Then came a pig—a 150-pound pig, one of the farm boys estimated. The pig seemed unconcerned though he had come straying out of the battle area. Lieutenant Feinstein had found a grass rope among some Jap stores which he wanted for a souvenir. He suggested to Kitcheon that they capture the pig in lieu of anything better to capture. 'And I will tie it by the neck,' Feinstein said. 'It won't work,' said Kitcheon. 'You can't hold pigs that way.' But he and Private First Class Raymond Cochran ran the pig down. Cochran caught it by the hind leg. The pig squealed and dragged him along the ground and everyone yelled. He and Kitcheon then roped it around the hind legs. In a few minutes it broke away and ran grunting to the rear. The men kidded Kitcheon and they began to wonder where the pig had come from."

Now I recognize that there is nothing here to make troops roll in the aisles and that the incident would have been far more funny if the man named Feinstein had tried to capture the pig, and the pig had responded by kicking him silly. Likewise, it would be a better story if the pig had proved to be the Japanese admiral trying to break through our lines in disguise.

On the other hand, I do insist that there is nothing here which would entitle a writer to try to make tears run down the civilian cheek. The men all thought it was funny. They laughed uproariously while Kitcheon was trying to capture the pig. Why shouldn't they have done so? They had just come through one skirmish in which a number of their own men had been killed and wounded. The chance to laugh was worth as much to them as a drink of strong wine. It is not selling human nature short to report that they made the most of it. Men in war are like men at home, in the office or on a golf course. They have the same natural responses to humor, to kindness, to friendship and to tears. It is when one begins to lack these things that he bears watching.

But there is one other part to the story. At the very moment when First Platoon was trying to capture the pig and was having a hilarious time doing it, Second Platoon, over on its left and about fifty yards away, was engaging in the fight against the Japanese-held spider holes, one of the bitterest and most deadly ordeals that I have ever known infantry to suffer. That fight went on for hours, with First Platoon knowing nothing of it, and in fact remaining so insensible to the general situation that they kept calling in derision to the Second Platoon: "Why don't you get off your ＿＿＿ ＿＿＿ and start fighting?"

So in the end I do not know whether I have more nearly proved Mr. Remarque's point or my own. He would say that the time wasted on the capture of a pig at Burton Island was stark tragedy because next door to that comic exhibition were unhelped, dying men who knew the final misery of loneliness in their worst hour. I would say that each part of the story must stand as it is, and that those who would understand the true nature of war must begin by understanding man's own nature, in its strength and in its weakness and in that fine balancing of good and evil, compassion amid brutality, hope amid ruins and laughter in the middle of death, which give man his unique capacity for survival.

We failed to capture the pig at Burton Island, and I can say nothing more of its fate. But for these and other reasons, I am ever ready to treat a pork chop kindly.

When Papa Took Paris

FROM war there is one story above others dear to my heart about which I have never written a line—the loony liberation of Paris.

There are reasons for this restraint: a promise once made; the unimportance of trying to be earnest about that which is ludicrous; the vanity of the hope that fact may ever overtake fiction; and the blight of the passing years on faded notes.

Then there is another thing—like a sweet dream, yesterday's rose or last month's pay, the event was gone before one could grasp it. From first to last it was as fantastic as *Uncle Tom* done by the late Cecil B. DeMille.

When the smoke cleared that night, nine of us dined at the Hôtel Ritz. Officially we were the only uniformed Americans in Paris. That knowledge made us more giddy than did the flow of champagne. There was food fit for the gods and service beyond price. But the head waiter made one ghastly blunder.

He slapped a Vichy tax on the bill. Straightaway we arose as one man and told him: "Millions to defend France, thousands to honor your fare but not one sou in tribute to Vichy."

He retired in confusion, crying: "It's the law!" and clutching a $100 tip. It was our finest and final victory of the evening. Then we did a round-robin signing of menu cards for the benefit of posterity. Among my souvenirs is the paper bearing the signatures of Colonel David K. E. Bruce, Brigadier General Edwin L. Sibert, Ernest Hemingway, Commander Lester Armour, USNR, G. W. Graveson, Captain Paul F. Sapiebra, Captain John G. Westover and J. F. Haskell. Above the signatures is the caption: "We think we took Paris."

But we agreed on something else. Hemingway said it: "None of us will ever write a line about these last twenty-four hours in delirium. Whoever tries it is a chump." On that pledge, we solemnly shook hands, raised our glasses, broke up and redeployed.

Still there had been a few touches which kept the show earthbound, encouraging the thought that we were not sleep-walking. For our column, the advance ended at the top of Avenue Foch in mid-afternoon. By then Paris was almost as free of gunfire as a modern July 4 picnic. So I walked on a hundred yards to get a front view of the Arc. At least 6000 cheering Parisians thronged the Étoile.

As I gazed upward, one last tank shell, out of nowhere, hit the outer edge of the stone pillar fifteen feet up. Of the effect on the crowd, there was no chance to judge. The square was absolutely empty before the echo died; the human tide simply evaporated. Not even a gendarme remained to cover the Eternal Flame.

Then I looked down the Champs hoping for a sign in keeping with the splendor of the hour. It was there all right, a great canvas ten feet deep, moored to the top stories of the buildings which faced the Arc and dominating the broad avenue. It read: "Hart, Schaffner & Marx Welcomes You," the final blessing on a great day. Next morning's promise was even brighter. By then a French AA gunner, from a battery which had set up next the Arc, had shot the sign down.

As all who visit Paris know, the Étoile is its bull's-eye. The great avenues radiate from it like spokes from a wheel hub. And the last street, as one approaches the Arc, Rue de Presbourg, makes a circle around the Étoile.

Toward the freeing of Paris, our final burst of sound and fury occurred along this roundabout. Save for cheering and the popping of champagne corks, the end of the drive along Avenue Foch had been quiet. Come to the circular street, the head of the column split and the French armor and halftracks deployed around it in both directions in a pincers movement perfectly designed to envelop the Unknown Soldier, had there been any resistance around him. Curious about the next move, I parked the jeep in front of No. 1 Avenue Foch and walked forward.

That was a mistake. Before I had passed two doors on Presbourg, the street was a gut of automatic and cannon fire which swept in both directions. The scars from that blast are still to be seen on the Presbourg walls. Some of it was random shooting aimed at nothing in particular. But several of the vehicles plainly were concentrating their fire on an apartment building opposite No. 1 Avenue Foch.

There was nothing to do but sink back into the nearest window embrasure, suck in my guts and hope for the best. Through the shot and shell came the Girl from Bilbao who figures in this story. She carried a carbine. She said: "I saw the weapon and knew that either you or John was unarmed. So I came looking." What a woman! I pulled her up into the embrasure and we stood there perfectly helpless.

This mad shooting went on for thirteen minutes. When it died, Paris began the return to normalcy which has lasted until now. I went looking for the French major commanding the forward tanks, simply to ask him: "What in hell are you doing?"

He said: "We're tranquilizing that enemy-held building."

I asked: "What enemy?"

His reply was positively fierce: "It is defended by the Japanese. We saw them at the window."

No answer was possible. It would have been as pointless to tell him that he was nutty as to accuse his troops of shooting up Paris real estate to enjoy an illusion of valor. But there was some argument for quitting his battalion at that moment and sitting on the curb.

The show was over. The tanks were moving on to a bivouac in another part of the city. The apartments lining the avenue were now spilling forth Frenchmen laden with pâtés, cold bottles and frozen grapes. And the jeep had taken two bullets from this last round of foolishness, one getting the windshield and the other a tire.

We drank. We ate. We glowed. And there was at least one bit of entertainment. Along the curb opposite, three Frenchmen and one woman suddenly ganged up on one female, rode her down into the street and were ready to apply scissors to her locks. It was too much for Sergeant Red Pelkey, Hemingway's driver. He was over there in a bound, kicking the hell out of the three men and shouting at the top of his voice: "Leave her alone, goddam you, you're all collaborationists!"

Amid such diversions, we still sat on the curb one hour later when we saw a small Oriental peering from the doorway of the bullet-riddled building across the street. He scuttled through the garden and collapsed just inside the gate. We walked to him. He was bleeding from a bullet crease in the shoulder but was more frightened than hurt.

I asked him: "Who are you?"

He replied: "Tonkinese—laundryman."

"What were you doing in the building?"

"Washing clothes."

"You looked from the building when the tanks went by?"

"Yes, I looked out to cheer parade."

So there it was. The major had been right, in a way. We put a first-aid pack on the little man. Unwittingly, he had been a hero of sorts—the last simulated spark of resistance to the Resistance.

Other scenes in this melodrama were no less mad. It is the only argument for beginning at the beginning, knowing that one will not be believed anyway.

The Village of Buc

Maybe Hannibal in front of Rome had as much good, clean fun. But I am inclined to doubt it. He had gone there on purpose and that rules him out. For I set it down as an almost inviolable principle that the truly good things which happen to you in war come by accident, like manna out of heaven, rather than because any earthly authority ordered or planned it that way.

Certainly, it was true of my connection with the liberating column. I didn't belong with the expedition and I had no intention of assigning myself to it for kicks. That's a fool's errand. The law of gravity determined the matter. I simply fell in and in the end couldn't get out.

I had been with the two United States airborne divisions, 82nd and 101st, in South England, completing my mission of determining what had happened to them in the Normandy drop. When I left them, they were already assembled in "The Bottoms" poised for a second jump into France. There was reason enough to accompany them since the show was certain to be entertaining.

But there was a more compelling argument for rejoining the 1st U.S. Army in the breakout, since I hadn't completed the account of the 1st Infantry Division's landing at Omaha Beach. The Big Red One had been put through the meat grinder; it was necessary to find out how and why it had happened. So on leaving my airborne friends, I promised that I would link up with their drop as promptly as possible, and then headed across the Channel, looking for whatever sector was held down by the 16th Infantry Regiment.

Now that was where Lady Luck began to take hold. The 16th Regiment was in line but its slice of the front was quiet, and it was obvious that my work could be completed quickly. On joining the Regiment, I happened to mention my other commitment to the regimental commander. There followed one week of debriefing his troops on the earlier operation. On the seventh day, at 9 A.M., I completed my notes and dismissed the last formation. It was time to thank the C.O. for his help.

Before I could open my mouth, he said: "I've got news for you. A flash just came in over the radio. Paris has just been liberated. Also, there has been an American air drop across the Seine. I suppose you want to hit the road."

We didn't take time to say goodbye. Westover, my man Friday, was already heading for the jeep. We took off in a cloud of dust. We didn't stop anywhere to check the reliability of this operational information. A good man had said it and we believed it; the thing was just as simple as that. That is how it happens in war. Natural impulse is ever the enemy of normal caution. The less fortunate die because of it. The hard facts were that there had been no air drop and Paris was still far from being liberated. But we had to learn these things through trial-and-error while luck ran a footrace with folly.

As the jeep chugged through a dozen or so liberated villages and snorted through the streets of Chartres, all sights and sounds were consistent with the morning's news. The ways were thronged with milling, enthusiastic crowds, buoyant as if on holiday. The highways were nigh choked with military transport, pushing slowly eastward as if drawn by a magnet. There were no MP's in sight, and seemingly no control points anywhere.

At the outskirts of Chartres a gentleman farmer flagged us down.

He said: "You have a funny army."

I said: "No funnier than any other army, but why do you think so?"

"Because it isn't allowed to drink milk."

"The hell it isn't; it drinks more milk than whisky."

"You're wrong. I brought out enough milk cans to take care of two battalions passing through. The first company was crazy about it. Then up came a major who told me your troops were not allowed to drink milk. So I hauled the rest of it back to the farm."

He was very sad. I wanted to console him. I said: "You see, old chap, we have in our country a purifying process. Our troops can't drink milk unless it is pasteurized."

At that point, he fairly wailed: "Why didn't they tell me? Pasteur was my grandfather. And you tell me how to purify milk?"

So naturally we rolled on away from there. And we had no way of knowing that before this show was over, we would have to conclude that the great scientist had pasteurized quite a tribe of Frenchmen.

At high noon we came to Rambouillet. We raced through without pausing for lunch or gas. In fact, we hadn't even noted the name. Six or seven miles past that fair city lies a small village named Buc. We got within one-quarter mile of it. We approached a wooded hill around which the road twists into the village.

I yelled to Westover: "Stop the jeep!"

He braked, then yelled back: "What's the matter, got the wind up?"

I said: "You're damned right. Did you ever hear anything as silent as this? Not a sound, anywhere along the road. And there isn't any wire laid along the road. Turn around and barrel. We're in enemy country."

That was what we did. Two miles to our rear, we bumped a battalion of French armor setting up a roadblock at a main intersection. I asked the commander: "Why are you going into position here?"

He said: "This is the front."

I asked: "Why don't you go on to Buc? There's a nice wooded hill just this side of it from where you can cover a spread of country."

He said: "That's the point. There are fifteen Tiger tanks on that hill partway dug in. We have spotted them from the air. But why fight them if you can turn them? I don't think we'll take that road to Paris. Nobody goes to Buc."

I said: "We went to Buc—or almost."

Intelligence Interlude

In a field echeloned slightly to the rear of the French tankers was an American unit, an antiair battery, one of 12th Army Group's stray chickens. Well, they ought to know something. We sauntered over and I asked the skipper: "What are you doing here?"

"Doing here?" As he echoed the words he sounded as if he wanted to have a good cry. "I don't even know where I am. So I decided to wait till somebody tells me."

"Sounds very sensible." Knowing no light was to be had from this quarter, we walked back to the roadblock crew. While we still talked to them, a jeep, mad with power, came racing into the crossroads from the direction of Versailles. It had to stop because the block was there. In it were two French civilians and a man in green twill who identified himself as a colonel of the OSS named Williams.

Williams said: "Howdy."

They had come from a rendezvous outside Paris in St.-Cloud with a group of Maquis who led the Paris resistance. Williams recounted the conversations and got finally to the raw meat: "It's all wrong about the city being liberated. This morning another 5000 SS arrived and joined the garrison. They intend to fight for it."

So this wasn't quite the afternoon for jumping a jeep across the Seine. One illusion had gone bang, though faith in the report of an American air drop near Paris still persisted.

Westover and I doubled back to Rambouillet with the idea of getting a cold bottle and victuals while pondering what to do next. On the edge of town we saw a Fighting French motor park and turned in with the sole object of putting the jeep under guard while we engaged a beer or two. It proved to be the headquarters of French 2nd Armored Division, which had beaten us to Rambouillet by an hour or so. We learned this when a colonel embraced me and introduced himself as General Leclerc's G-2.

He asked: "Where have you come from?"

Stretching things a bit, I said: "From Buc."

"Impossible!" he replied. "No one has been to Buc."

So then I told him all that I had heard from his own people and ours—the presence of the enemy tanks at Buc, the position of his roadblock, the news given by Williams that Paris was far from liberated.

The Colonel's eye gleamed. He said: "I must take you to Leclerc. You must tell him all. This is major intelligence."

I said: "My dear Colonel, you could get on a bicycle, ride down that road for about an hour and learn everything I have told you. But you won't find Colonel Williams. He headed south, looking for a bath. He says he is very dirty."

He said: "My friend, this is more than we have heard all day. You would be surprised at the distance separating my desk from what I need to know."

Though in the telling the incident seems absurd, the grain of comfort is that in the doing it seemed tenfold sillier. Thus dragooned, we met Leclerc, who even in his fly-ridden tent looked and acted like a miniature Mars. Of this dedicated and courageous fighter for France, untimely killed by a peacetime air crash in Sahara, many hands have written, and my experiences with him were so brief that nothing worth-while may be added.

What stays in my memory is as vague as the impression of a Cheshire cat minus the grin. The figure was trim and dressed as if for a skirmish. The face was abnormally pink, the eye steely cold and the mustache clipped close to vanishing. While I talked he stood rigid, not even flexing a face muscle. Well, no, that is not quite correct.

As I reached the point of saying: ". . . and according to Williams there are five thousand newly arrived SS in the city who will fight for it," for the first time Leclerc relaxed. Putting his hand on my arm, he smiled radiantly, pointed an index finger toward heaven and said: "Have no fear! I, Leclerc, shall smash them!"

It was a wonderful pitch and quite suddenly I came awake to it. The Colonel had introduced me as Historian of the United States Army. Leclerc was talking for the benefit of Clio the Muse of History.

So I got out my little notebook and I wrote down his immortal words, which are here reported for the first time. On several occasions during the advance I saw and talked to Leclerc again but his words were no longer on parade. What he had said was good enough; they typify him; they could serve as his epitaph. His assured presence was an antidote to the contagion of fear and he smashed the enemies of France at every point where he could lay on.

That was the end of the conversation. Suffice to add that the urge to drop pearls for harvesting by future generations is not peculiar to Frenchmen or limited to their generals. The trouble is that few have the inspired brevity to match Major General Ralph Smith's gem of an official message when he reported the conquest of his assigned island in the Gilberts: "Makin taken."

In the heart of Rambouillet was an ancient hotel delightfully shaded. There Ernest Hemingway had held forth during the preceding several days while the town was being defended by a group of FFI. Colonel David K. E. Bruce of the OSS, later U.S. Ambassador to the Court of St. James, was with him. Together, they supervised the irregular operations around Rambouillet, while American units maneuvered in the general neighborhood but did not close on

Rambouillet. Many tall tales have been written about Force Hemingway. The real story is good enough. As a war writer, Hemingway spun fantastic romance out of common yarn. But he had the courage of a saladang and he was uncommonly good at managing guerillas.

That afternoon he was away from the hotel. Its surrounding apple orchard swarmed with bees darting at the honeysuckle and big-name war correspondents attacking the apples. There was enough talent in that plot to cover Armageddon.

Ernie Pyle was there, a bit unsteady, a little teary. It was our last conversation. No, he wasn't going for Paris, the hell with Paris. He said: "I'm leaving here to go home. I can't take it any longer. I have seen too many dead. I wasn't born for this part. It haunts me. I'll never go to war again. I'll never let anyone send me. I'll quit the business first."

A great little guy. But hardly clairvoyant.

Matter of Sentiment

We are still at Rambouillet. What I did not know when I talked to General Leclerc and found him ignorant of his situation was that he had been on the road most of that day with his Division, barreling from Argentan, which is a hellish long haul for armor.

Here it is desirable to backtrack and explain why things happened in the way they did. To jump from the small picture in the Rambouillet apple orchard to the grand design ordered from on high is appropriate to the liberating operation. It had no continuity and its reckonings were made, as a submariner would say, by guess and by God.

There was in Paris a M. Gallois, leader of an especially aggressive resistance group. In mid-August his forces had started pushing the Germans around, driving them from building to building by fire. The situation became so acute that the Germans asked for a truce, starting the night of 20 August and continuing until noon on 25 August. The fact was that General Von Cholitz, their commander, did not have his heart in the defense and was stalling for a break which would relieve him of his embarrassment without scuttling his honor.

Because of the truce, M. Gallois jumped the gun, taking it for granted that the job was done and Paris was delivered. That was how the rumor became floated out of a semi-solid foundation. Like Revere, Gallois mounted his horse and rode to carry the word, heading for General Patton's 3rd Army.

From its headquarters, he was passed by Colonel La Belle, the liaison officer, to the 12th Army Group's CP. The G-2, Brigadier General Edwin L. Sibert, took what Gallois had told him and went by plane to carry the story to Generals Eisenhower and Bradley, who were in that hour conferring.

On getting the news, Bradley said to Eisenhower: "Let's send the French 2nd Armored in." That is how the decision was made, according to Sibert, the eyewitness, and that is how it was done.

Being at Argentan, at least three days' hard driving from the target city, Leclerc's force was not in the most favorable position to move up swiftly and close the gap created by 3rd Army's bypassing of the Paris area. The vacuum around Rambouillet, which Hemingway's bulk had partly plugged, was a happenstance of the wait while Leclerc came up.

General Omar N. Bradley, for all his native shrewdness and hard practicality as an operator, is at heart a sentimentalist. Months before, while in Africa, he had promised that if he could have his way, when the hour came to free Paris, Frenchmen would do it. He perhaps did not anticipate that it would be his responsibility to call the shots. Still, he remembered.

However, if the High Command shared in full the supreme optimism of M. Gallois, it still left very little to chance. The jury-rigged plan which developed around the main idea of passing the laurel to Leclerc's division was framed with due caution. Its parts made Leclerc's advance a major reconnaissance in force, rather than a road march, designed to test whether the Germans intended to stand and fight before backing away.

Leclerc got his orders at Argentan on a Tuesday afternoon. His division was to move to the northwest rim of Paris and there demonstrate. The clear purpose was to threaten and abort the garrison under Von Cholitz if possible, rather than to engage it. For in the subsequent move, still not entering Paris, the French armor was to make a great wheel around to the southwest of the city, then force an entry in the neighborhood of Sèvres. In so doing, it should snare most of the game.

The United States 4th Infantry Division was then a few miles southwest of Lonjuneau and much closer to Paris. The plan proposed for it a kind of backstop role, to move but not to fight, to hang its clothes on a hickory limb but not go near the water. Major General Barton's mission was supposed to be complete when his command "seized high ground south of Paris," there to shout yoo-hoo at the Eiffel Tower across magnificent distance.

The 4th got its orders on the afternoon of 23 August, by which time Leclerc was already closing on Rambouillet, approximately equidistant from the heart of Paris. The timing was perfect. From the topside view it must have looked as if everything was set.

Nothing intervened to spoil the script except its own unsuitability. The architects had thought of the liberation as a normal military operation rather than as a what's-it for which the TV people have since coined the label "a spectacular." The plan simply frustrated the desire of the French to fight for their capital even more than it miscalculated the readiness of Germans to give them the opportunity.

Leclerc's assigned mission fell apart when he got word of the substantial force of German armor covering the road at Buc. He might have brushed off this block by bringing up the artillery or calling for an air strike.

But now there was a palpable reason for changing direction, declining the oblique maneuver to the northwest, and by wheeling farther south, insuring that he would have to take his division directly into the city. In a very real sense, by momentarily risking the appearance that he was avoiding a fight, he was gambling that he would get a real

one. There were supreme values of the spirit in that decision. Who may say that he was wrong? More than others,
soldiers need to be reminded that freedom has to be won
every day.

However, the change altered the whole frame of operations, whether because High Command got an exaggerated
impression of German strength or became dubious when
Leclerc took the direct approach. On the next day, U.S.
4th Infantry Division was ordered to go directly into Paris
instead of cooling on the outside. Everybody loves a race. So
it happened that 4th's spearhead—one battalion of the
12th Infantry Regiment—got to Notre Dame at noon on the
big day just as Leclerc was crossing the Seine. History
doesn't say so, but history is often wrong.

The En Avant

When in field operations a man jellies on the pivot, wondering what next to do, anything moving in what seems to be the right direction pulls like a magnet. That is how we happened to join General Leclerc's column headed for Paris. Busy man, he had neglected to invite us. Otherwise, he had been most courteous. But this was not his manner toward all men on that day. According to the legend which blooms larger every time any magazine writer dwells on Hemingway and war, he got to Leclerc and told him how to fight his battle and where to expect resistance. There's no doubt that the contact was made. But as to what came of it, Hemingway should be the best witness. He wrote: "We advanced in some state toward the General. His greeting—unprintable—will live in my ears forever. 'Buzz off, you unspeakables,' the gallant general said in effect in something above a whisper. Colonel Bruce, the resistance king, and your armored-operations correspondent hastily withdrew."

In the free-for-all situation, we had no orders. In late evening, we still dallied in the Hôtel du Grand Veneur in Rambouillet, having almost given up the idea of joining the air drop across the Seine because the Germans obstinately blocked the road. Four tanks and ten halftracks passed the veranda, French-manned and headed east. Westover said: "Maybe they're going to bull through to Paris. Maybe that story about the RB at Buc is bunk. Maybe we ought to get going." So with no more thought than that we mounted the jeep and trailed after. The attachment was made *ad hoc* and was not thereafter questioned. The blue card which I carried entitling me to move anywhere I pleased in the Theatre stayed in my pocket.

But it was only a short turn with no encores. The column veered south from the road we had earlier traveled, and after a half-dozen miles pulled up in a wood southwest of Cernay-la-Ville. It was the division bivouac. In the forest of Fighting French, one almost missed the trees. Enough light remained to pitch the pup tent. That night nothing happened except steady rain and the arrival of an unsteady American major. He was from the staff of U.S. V Corps but had somehow lost it. His tone was like a child deserted by Mama.

Westover said to him: "The hell with V Corps. This show is headed for Paris. Come along and you'll have the time of your life. If you're already lost, two days more won't hurt. Besides, the boss knows General Gerow and he'll square it for you."

The major said a few noble words about duty, then settled down, sleeping under his own jeep. When we were awakened at dawn by hundreds of Frenchmen booming like bitterns throughout the wood, he was all enthusiasm. How could one avoid it? All around us were warriors scuttling about with the eccentric motion of waterbugs, pounding their chests and screaming: *"En avant!"* Lasting all of ten minutes, that cry pulled us right out of our sacks, and when at last everyone grew hoarse, we "enavanted."

By breakfast time we were already into Cernay-la-Ville, the first town liberated along the Paris road. It was nice timing. Dear ladies, young and old, came running from their homes with platters of fried eggs, rolls and coffee. I remember it as a little holiday of generous tears and laughter, unmarred by the crude words of one young punker: "Happy to see you. Give me one pack cigarettes for my papa. We have waited long."

At Cernay, Westover put the jeep around the main body of the armor and we joined the advance guard as it marked time on a hillside beyond the village. Again we marched. Chevreuse was already behind us and the advance guard, made up of a few jeeps and four halftracks, was approaching the airport at Toussus-le-Noble when we heard the artillery speak the first time. It was a novel situation. The column stopped in a defile where the road twisted through and over a narrow valley as steep-sided as a ravine. We could neither back away nor deploy. Off to our left we counted twenty-three muffled explosions. To me they signified nothing consequential.

I said: "They're going out."

Westover said: "Wrong, boss, they're coming in. There's something up ahead of us."

And of course I knew he had to be right about it. Over forty years my hearing, though acute to most else, has never been attuned to the pitch of artillery shell. I'm tone deaf to explosions, though I don't know why. Westover knew the sounds like a maestro knows his scale. He had been a forward observer in Italy before I got him. Even in his sleep his subconscious told him the difference between outgoing and incoming noise. With our own guns pounding next his ear, he snored happily on; but one incoming round bursting anywhere near would bring him awake. It was a joy to have him around.

Behind us, at some distance, a few French guns countered perfunctorily. Then we lurched on. Nothing ahead had been reconnoitered, but when *en avant* is the watchword, prudence has no virtue. By the time the advance guard topped the rise we had company. The lead battalion, a motorized unit riding trucks and attended by armor, had closed the interval and was right on our heels. The one road cut straight through the center of the airport. The lead of the column was riding virtually bumper to bumper as we drove along this causeway. We got midway. The passage was still a defile.

On either side of us, the fields which had been an airport, where they were not bomb-cratered, were an impassable morass. Either go ahead or stall—there was no other choice.

It was stall. But not by choice. From directly in front of us, on a beeline, and not more than 1100 yards away, an artillery piece suddenly spoke German. The whizzbang effect said it was an 88. Then ditto, ditto, ditto. Our little tinclad van was rolling directly into the teeth of an enemy battery. From rightward of the battery somewhere a 105-mm also opened fire, and from left of it a heavy machine gun spat and sputtered.

These latter items were small change. But the fire from the 88's was a fast strike down the middle. The truck three lengths ahead of us was hit dead on. Then a jeep thirty paces to the rear got smacked.

It wasn't the right time to get out. We'd already made it. I had jumped to the slope of a drainage ditch which paralleled the road. Being more agile, Westover had vaulted it and was in a bomb crater beyond. As for the major from U.S. V Corps, he had jack-knifed beautifully straight into the muck of the ditch bottom. He arose looking like a refugee from a sewer. He said: "I've been thinking it over. It was wrong of me to come along. I must return to my duty." He turned his jeep around and somehow managed to swing out past the stalled armor. We never saw him again, but he was a love while we had him.

No one has ever managed to diagnose the emotions of fish in a barrel. It could have been that bad but only momentarily. The shelling continued. But the German battery was getting nervous. Its stuff began going wild. Westover was much more comfortable in his bomb crater than was I, flattened on the bank of the roadside ditch. Since the battery was aiming straight down the road and the ditch ran parallel to it, clear to the guns, its bank offered only that relative mental peace which an infantryman knows when he tries to hide behind a one-inch sapling under shell-

fire, rather than sit, no more exposed, absolutely in the open. Not how things are but how they seem makes the difference between a tight clutch on the straw of security and a surrender to despair. Westover was happy enough in his muddy crater but I knew we were not going to stay there; his horse-laugh in my direction rang too loudly.

Forward along the road 150 yards, and that much closer to the battery, was a ruined building, partly wrecked by earlier air bombings and now smoking from a hit by the battery. But its stone walls still stood and beckoned. There lay sanctuary from the spite of the enemy, and even more from his noise. My aversion to that particular dual-purpose gun dates from 1918 when we called such "Austrian 88's." The whizzbang impact on the senses even in that day made 88 fire seem as personally aimed as the derringer bullet which shot Mr. Lincoln. Except for a one-pounder, nothing is more demoralizing.

So I yelled to Westover: "See that building! That's where we're going. Get moving!" As we slogged along, the battery fire seemed to be drifting off, as if the frightened gunners were reprieving the stalled column just when they had it dead to rights.

Nothing in life is stranger than the way in which a new association of ideas may quite suddenly change one's emotions toward a particular object, thought or strain of music and fix them steadfastly for all time. Until the war I had abominated Debussy's "Clair de Lune." It had been the theme song of the soap opera "Mary Marlin," or one such, and like all gems in a huckster setting, had been well tarnished.

Not knowing it, I was at the point of change as we drew near the wrecked building. Its immediate setting and some brightness in the decor bespoke that it had been a café. One shell from the battery had knocked the sign from above the door some minutes earlier. We turned it over. It said "Clair de Lune." In the years since I have loved this piece

Road to the German Battery

of music steadily and passionately. Had we not turned over the sign and read, my feelings would be as before. But there was a charmed hour within the strong walls of that old café, though why its minutes were high I cannot say, except that they were sweet and friendly, and they became the portal to a delirious adventure.

Inside, the café was what reporters describe as a shambles, though I have never bothered to learn what a shamble might be. Part of the wall was blown in. The furniture was all either smashed or overturned. The floor was littered with empty bottles, shattered china and cruets. The air hung heavy with the mingled aromas of horse manure and stale beer.

While we looked and poked about, hopeful of finding a name brand to be plucked from the burning, from under the overturned bar came the low-throated chuckle of a woman. There was something very pleasant about it, as if she were laughing at us, not because we looked funny but because that was the best way to greet another human.

We turned the bar upright and she stood. It is enough to say how she looked on first sight since she did not later change. She was small and slight and much too ill-clad and dirty to be described as a gracious figure. Her dark face was marred by conspicuously bucked teeth. The eyes were brown almost to blackness. Her hair was tangled and hung stringily halfway to her waist. Her gown looked like a cut-down Mother Hubbard, once black, faded to gray and frequently slept in. Such was Elena and she was just 18. But no unkempt damsel ever wore a warmer and less embarrassed smile. I will give Elena that, adding also that her courage made her seem beautiful during the two days we knew her.

The reason for these rough-hewn details is that the great American novelist was later to picture her as a gorgeously bewitching siren who held every man of the column in the hollow of her classic hand. Also, he made of her a profound philosopher, spouting great words about noble causes, whereas I have known few women who have had such an appalling gift of reticent silence. That was for *Collier's* but it was also for the birds. Elena was, as I have set her forth, simple and unbeautiful. Hemingway hadn't yet stumbled into this scene but he was on his way in search of a friendly wall. Outside, the stalled armor was still taking a pasting from the battery. It was good to be inside.

Elena's first words were: "What is American opinion of Marshal Pétain?" So help me—that was what she said even before she had tugged at a stocking or straightened her dress. A most unusual woman, though the strangeness of her mental processes was no more startling than the irregularity of her speech. A light dawned. Since her French conjugation was almost as abominable as my own, she too must be a stranger.

I said in Spanish: "You are not French?" (We never got around to saying how Pétain rated back home.) She grinned proudly and replied: "I'm from Bilbao. I came here to fight with the resistance. My man is FFI. He's somewhere out in front of this column."

As she said it, Hemingway came through the door. We had last talked at Key West in 1936. But it could have been yesterday. Like Elena, Ernest wasn't saying any onstage words for history. As if the sun would also rise, or there might be death in the afternoon, depending on the answer, he yelled: "Marshall, for God's sake, have you got a drink?" But the bells were not yet tolling for him. I said: "We've ransacked this place; we don't have; we have not."

Westover spoke: "Boss, there's a fifth of Scotch in your pack back in the jeep. You put it there three weeks ago and forgot it." I said: "OK, Big Mouth, for having such a good memory you can walk back through that fire and get it." He did.

One of the minor surprises of war is the great thirst of any group of fugitives from the law of averages. With Elena helping—I had just introduced her to Hemingway—that soldier was dead within twenty minutes. So by then were quite a few members of the German battery, the French artillery having at last gotten the range.

But that isn't how the story came out in *Collier's*. Here's how Ernest saw it: "I took evasive action and waded down the road to a bar. Numerous guerillas were seated in it singing happily and passing the time of day with a lovely Spanish girl from Bilbao whom I had last met at Cognieres. This girl had been following wars and preceding troops since she was fifteen and she and the guerillas were paying no attention to the *accrochage* at all. A guerilla chief named C asked me to have a drink of his excellent white wine." Ah there's romance, and isn't it fun to be a pack of guerillas once in a lifetime? Who'd have thought it?

Too late for him, early enough for us, we were joined by a remarkable character with the *nom de guerre* of "Mouton," leader of the local FFI. His real name was Michel

Pasteur. This particular descendant of the great scientist was about thirty-five, tall and spare, with flaming red hair and sky-blue eyes. He had the stride, carriage and dress of a hog drover. Beyond his courage, Mouton's overawing asset was his silence. He had maximized the art of making himself understood by means of variously intoning a grunt. It wasn't his fault exactly that in the Hemingway stories about the liberating of Paris, Mouton became the reincarnated Demosthenes. Somebody had to put words in his mouth or they'd never have made it.

Mouton grunted, belched and pointed to the leftward. We took it to mean that we were to prowl outward through the ruined hangars toward the German machine gun to see if it was still cooking with gas. By then we were all feeling hardy as lions. Hemingway said: "If we get in any trouble, I will take care of you," which gave Westover such a giggle that he almost split his Silver Star ribbon. Such cracks were a habit with Ernest, due to his owning the copyright on war. There were other reasons why he was called Papa but this one was good enough.

Because of the slough, the knocked-over hangars and the wreckage of the two B-17's, we didn't get very far very fast, and finally the way was blocked wholly. It was then that Hemingway said: "I think we ought to patrol all the way if you're up to it." Mouton grunted. Again Westover laughed. Together, we shagged back to Clair de Lune and there was no further mention of patrolling.

It was all so like Papa. He would still have tried to amble forward had anyone picked up his idea; that he might have been shot for his pains was immaterial. He loved soldiering, with reservations. Being in an armed camp exhilarated him and he had a natural way with the military. The excitement and danger of battle were his meat and drink, just as the unremitting obligation to carry on was his poison.

To put it more accurately, he loved playing at soldier on the grand scale, with shooting irons. Yet in him, it was not a juvenile attitude. I truly believe he played at it because he enjoyed the game more than because he was interested in studying men under high pressure. There was this difference in view between us. I have always looked at war as a matter-of-fact business, requiring the rejection of every unnecessary risk and the facing of any danger along the path of duty. A man fully aware of his genius can afford more than that.

There was sudden motion at the front of the column. No signal came to us at the wrecked café but it was in the air that we were about to move again.

Hemingway said: "What about the girl?"

"Well, what about her?"

He said: "She can't be left here. The countryside remains in German hands. The column is only mopping up a highway. Leave her here and she may be killed or captured."

That was how we came to welcome Elena aboard the jeep and why it happened that a Spanish girl held high the first American flag that went into Paris. I was not under General Leclerc's orders, he didn't dare bounce me, and no one else felt safe to lift her. We suddenly acquired a traveling companion and Hemingway made a first sighting of a love theme for another story about men in war.

The column was still in a defile, made so by the quagmire on both sides of the road where once had been an air field. In the van of the column were jeeps and trucks. Perhaps 500 yards forward of the first vehicle, the earth flanking the road became solid. There we could fan out and deploy in line. The German battery was still firing feebly, and with the occasional rounds from the 88's was mixed some supporting stuff from one automatic gun and a few rifles.

Out of this unique situation came the weirdest order of attack that I have ever seen in any military operation. We advanced with jeeps in line first, followed by trucks in line, followed by halftracks, followed by tanks. In the emergency there was no other way to thin out the formation. Then as the unarmored vehicles began to spread over the open fields, the halftracks and tanks, gripping on solid ground, would swing out and around, pinching in toward the battery from both sides.

That is how it was done, and looking back now, I would say that had any safer, saner movement been possible, it would not have suited the hilarious nature of that thoroughly madcap adventure. One touch of orthodoxy would have been as out of keeping as a gravestone at a wedding.

From where we rode, the prospect could be faced cheerfully. We were the next to the last jeep with the advance guard. The road ahead, at the point where the extension would begin, was shaded by a straight line of Lombardy poplars all the way to the battery and slightly inside of it. So when the other jeeps deployed, we could hold the road and hug the line of the trees. It was a very satisfactory bumper guard now that the battery was dying.

Silly as it sounds, the thing went off well. We were within 500 yards of the guns when the finish came. The tanks and halftracks completed their sweep, firing like crazy. No flag was waved. No shout was heard. Suddenly we saw twenty or thirty men come out of that nest and stagger across the open field toward us, hands in air. Only one man couldn't, because one hand and the other arm had been shot away. Still, he reeled along. Others were bleeding from the chest, head, shoulder, and legs. These things we saw as we drew abreast of them.

But no one minded or paid the slightest heed. They were walking emptily into nothingness and we were again back to the road with everyone straining toward Paris. Some must have continued this march macabre until they perished from bleeding. Than this, I have seen few uglier sights in combat.

French Without Tears

That sudden decision to pick up Elena and take her to Paris, made as lightly as one plucks a kitten from a puddle, had unlimited romantic consequences, not at the moment foreseeable.

Elena was the innocent catalyst rather than the prime mover. We lacked a spare helmet or knitted cap, the jeep was topless, and with her long tresses floating in the breeze as we buzzed along, there was no way to disguise her. For that day of razzle-dazzle fire and movement, she was a conspicuous heroine, the lone woman in a column of armored Frenchmen, all bent on playing Cyrano or maybe D'Artagnan.

But night must fall and Frenchmen must think of other things than war. By the hour a late moon found us bivouacked in the gutters opposite the Renault plant on the wrong side of the Seine, there was not a tank, halftrack or truck in the column but bloomed with women. Each frowning turret looked like a beauty-parlor ad, and the squealing within and around the hulls did not come of grit in the bogie wheels. Leclerc's mobile division had suddenly doubled in size while losing half of its fight power, which is a modern miracle. Higher officers tried to do something about it. Men pointed to the river as if to say: "Go jump!"

There were other attachments than Elena, less embarrassing but not more mysterious. At Toussus-le-Noble, a number of U.S. correspondents got up to the advance guard.

I remember few names and faces but I think Jack Belden, Beaver Thompson and Ken Crawford were in this sortie. Leclerc just didn't like newsmen, though he loved historians. One of his staff colonels tried to give these heroes the bum's rush, shouting that they lacked orders.

I said: "Turn them over to me and I'll be responsible."

The Colonel protested: "But you have no troops!" and when I said: "But that will give me some," he more or less folded.

However, he got in one parting shot: "You will report on them regularly!" which was wonderful, inasmuch as I never saw any of them again, except Hemingway. He stayed close. The others wandered off looking for this or that and some got the heave-ho from the French as soon as they passed from sight.

I will get back to the calmer workaday entries from my diary of the loony liberation soon enough. There is one concluding note on the feminization of the French 2nd Armored. Five days after the liberation was complete, Leclerc was still trying to get the women of Paris out of his tanks. The division bivouac in the fields out along the Soissons road looked like a transplanted Pig Alley under arms. Somewhere along the line the crews had formed a bad habit and I do not doubt it was all Elena's fault.

Memory's a witch. Thinking back, I would have sworn that the German battery at Toussus was overwhelmed in a breeze with no loss to our side. But thumbing through my faded notes I find this entry: "As we advance, one French halftrack, turning into the battery, is hit dead on. Ahead of me an overloaded weasel takes a direct hit from a shell. Our losses, six killed and 11 wounded." Possibly someone paused to give first aid. But I did not see it. We who witnessed their misery strained only to return to the road again and get on. Most of the day was like that. Normal reactions were numbed by the overpowering urge to keep moving. The pell-mell nature of the advance produced an hypnosis which dulled the mind to sights and sensations.

We churned on to Jouay-en-Josas. There the column blocked and stopped as the van started uphill through the main street. We were hard by the railway station and for five minutes the wait was joyous. Out poured the townsfolk, their arms loaded with cold bottles of champagne. Mothers lifted babies to be kissed, only to be crowded out by the younger beauties of the place who had the same general idea. Old soldiers, who looked like relics of the Franco-Prussian War, lined the sidewalks standing at stiff salute.

Then the music started. The Germans had a heavy mortar battery in a nearby château and behind it two field guns. They had the right notion but lacked the range. A few rounds hit the town church. Others landed on a wooded knoll immediately to our backs, without visible effect except to increase the flow of bubbly. Three French tanks charged the battery position; one was knocked out, the others finished the action.

We moved up to Main Street and again halted. Twenty-one German prisoners, several of them wounded, all of them captured in the fight around the château, were brought back to be paraded single-file down the Main Street of Jouay-en-Josas. About sixty Frenchmen of the advance guard formed facing each other within the street, holding aloft their rifles, mess gear or any hard object that was swingable. As the Germans entered this gauntlet, they cracked down hard, aiming at the heads of the passing men. The Germans didn't try to run. They marched. Except where they reeled or fell from a blow, they took it heads-up, eyes to the front, saying not a word, uttering no cry. They emerged from it looking as if they had been torn by wild beasts. There was wretched and unforgettable depravity in this scene, redeemed only by the bearing of a few helpless young men who knew how to walk seemingly without fear. To have tried to intervene would have been bolder than any act I saw along the road to Paris.

We were in motion again, and shortly we made a sharp right turn onto a main avenue three kilometers east of Versailles. The road ahead was a mass of greenery, its surface blocked by a half-mile long line of felled sycamore trees. At the far end was a conspicuous block formed of two overturned trucks banked with rocks and timber.

The leading French tanks moved uncertainly into this stuff and shunted away the first half of it while we, in the jeep, idled. Four hundred yards off to our left was a dense copse covering an area the shape and size of a city block. Out of it suddenly a man came running, screaming into the wind.

I asked Elena: "What's he saying?"

She said: "There's a German anti-aircraft battery in that wood. Three guns altogether. And they're ready to open fire."

So with the way partly cleared, we sped ahead, looking for the commander of the forward tank battalion to tell him he was about to be smacked broadside. And we made it— or almost.

Through Elena, I told him. Nothing had yet happened. With every second counting, he still might have gotten his tanks around. At least he listened respectfully. Then he answered: "I know all about it; we've already taken care of that battery."

Never was an overconfident statement more beautifully punctured. It came like this—Boom! Boom! Boom!—right on our rear. At 400 yards point-blank the Germans couldn't miss. Behind us there was loud screaming. One vehicle on the pivot exploded. Another burst into flame. Said the French Major: "So now we know."

So much for the legend that intelligence supplied by Hemingway, with an assist from his two adjutants, Mouton and David Bruce, enabled Leclerc and troops to slip through to Paris, skirting the nodules of resistance. Nothing nastier could be said of them; not one sign of applied intelligence distinguished the operation. We careened through the countryside as witlessly as a convoy of boob bandits trying to shake off the law.

During this and the succeeding scenes, our great and gentle friend, Papa, was close beside us, right to the finish. Blessed be his memory, and hallowed his reputation for fighting gumption, they should not be sullied with canards such as this, quoted from one American magazine:

"Behind Papa's jeep wheezed the long line of Renault sedans, taxis, jalopies and trucks, all of them crammed with Task Force Hemingway's fighters, now numbering more than 200. 'We'll tag along with Leclerc as far as Buc,' Papa said, 'then near Versailles where our information shows we will be slowed down by resistance, we'll swing around and come into Paris by a back road one of our bike boys found. The chief of staff didn't think the road was quick enough, but I do.' Just as Hemingway anticipated, Leclerc was temporarily pinned down along the south bank of the Seine by a small group of determined Nazis left behind by the retreating Germans. When Leclerc finally overwhelmed the resistance, his advance patrols moved into Paris. The Germans had deserted the city. As Leclerc entered he noticed a large sign hanging from the door of a cathedral: 'Property of Ernest Hemingway.' "

Well, glory and hallelujah. Papa stayed with us, then and later, never breaking away toward Versailles. His only attachment was Sergeant Red Pelkey, his jeep driver. Leclerc's boys acted like nitwits, but if they were slowed anywhere by resistance, it came from the mademoiselles, not the krauts. Papa deserves more credit than he has been given; he was not one to force his talents beyond their natural limits.

Our final lurch, after the column had swung past Orly Field and then, turning leftward, entered the solidly built-up area south of the Seine, took 24 hours. Tactically, there seemed to be no good reason for it. I have always suspected that we dragged feet while the stage managers tried to better the arrangements for the grand entry. Anyone, at any time, may enjoy the illusion of capturing Paris after dark.

Through the whole ride we were as perverse as possible. We tore madly along when reason whispered that we should proceed with care. We stalled insensibly whenever the way seemed wide open. It was less a fighting operation than a carnival on wheels. Take what happened after the German battery, concealed in the copse just off our flank, ripped the column broadside. Rather quickly, tank fire killed that battery. Yet we did not turn back to see how much damage had been done to the people behind us. On the run forward, the jeep had pulled up between two medium tanks. In the shuffling which attended the exchange of fires, the tank behind us moved forward a few yards. It became impossible to turn. Then both tanks resumed the advance and we went along between them willy-nilly, rather than be run down. This proved embarrassing. Forward one-half mile our route turned left, at which point we headed straight toward the Seine.

Right at the junction, with the closest piled explosives only 20 feet from the road we must take, was a block-long German ammunition dump. The stacked shells were already blowing sky-high, and even at a distance, the smoke, blast and flame seemed like inferno. For that, we could thank the killed-off German battery. With a final round or two it had fired the dump just before being knocked out of action. In so doing, it had blocked the road, or to put it more precisely, that was what we supposed for the moment.

The lead tanks came to the intersection. There was not even a pause for a close-up view of the danger. They wheeled left and advanced in file right across the face of the exploding dump. Its metal showered the roadway and its heat was like a blast from molten slag.

For the people within the tanks the risks were trivial. They had battened their hatches and the plate was thick enough to withstand the hot fragments. They did not take it on the run as they should have done; they snailed along at about six miles per hour.

I yelled: "We can't make that run."

Westover yelled: "We've got to, or the tanks will crush us. They're not stopping for anything."

That's how it was. The jeep-loaded people spliced into the tank column were held feet-to-the-fire by their own friends. That Mazeppa ride lasted not more than forty or fifty seconds by the clock, but the clock lied. There was no protection against either the flying metal or the infernal heat. The best one could do was cover his face with his arms, double up so as to compose as small a target as possible—and hope for the best.

Being on the outside, the jeep drivers had a little more insulation, but being drivers, they had to sit more or less erect to keep the vehicle on the road. So everything evened up and nobody had it very good. Those were moments to be remembered. As here described, the thing may sound worse than it in fact was but no sappier than it then seemed. Or is that really accurate? Was the folly of it given even a passing thought? In the swift transition attending a suddenly arisen danger there is not even time for fear to down the first surge of wild excitement. That is true of running into ambush in the jungle. The shaking comes later.

We pulled out of it whole-skinned. One shard had smashed through the hood of the jeep. Another had smacked the metal panel next the jump seat missing Elena's bottom by inches. The quarter-ton still perked. It was hellishly hot and we were horribly thirsty.

There was not far to go. Where the dump ended, the metropolitan city began. In a twinkling, we were among houses and stores and banking both sides of that broad, lovely avenue were the people—and what a people!

They had waited four years for this parade and they were ready with the *vin d'honneur* and much more. There were again the Old Guard standing at salute, wearing faded képis and fresh-shined medals, young mothers rushing out with infants to be kissed, more beautiful blondes and brunettes, and some not so lovely, platoons of urchins screaming and frantically raising their hands in the V-signal, dear old gammers showing their petticoats when they raised their skirts to weep, and everywhere, men and women, shouting, laughing, crying and embracing one another in ecstatic delirium.

It was about then that Westover pulled a folded Star-Spangled flag from his pack, mounted it on a pup-tent pole and gave it to Elena to hold high. That small gesture of pure patriotism was the great mistake. Right then the unattached females along the march route began climbing into Leclerc's tanks and halftracks to stay. Elena had challenged them. It was time to strike a blow for France. And they didn't have any flags.

There was no way to refuse that mass of mad humanity. So there were countless stops and starts by the column. Repeatedly, the people surged onto the avenue and stood solid until the armor ground to a halt. But when they rushed the vehicles, it was not to pour champagne, cognac and calvados. They dumped the bottles whole, the champagne chilled, the hard stuff still uncorked. When the jeep at last reached the bank of the Seine, like coals to Newcastle, it was carrying 67 bottles of champagne on a run into Paris. To cap the climax, we gave it back to other Frenchmen. Like I say, everyone was a little cuckoo.

Papa Hemingway was still with us, and very busy, not instructing the FFI scouts, advising Leclerc or bending the elbow. Like a happy tourist, he was snapping pictures of everyone and anything in sight.

That night we bivouacked on the broad avenue, 100 yards short of the Pont de Sèvres, directly across the Seine from the Renault plant. From the Longchamps race track, the German artillery tried to bring the column under fire but the closest shells hit high on the ridge running off in the direction of Versailles. Through the night our tank destroyers returned the fire from positions along the river bank. One flight of German bombers came over and misdropped a few eggs. It happened at midnight and the explosions were hardly audible above the tumult in the street.

The Last Hurrah

All morning long the column chewed its nails but we couldn't cross the bridge before we came to it. The generals behaved like union men honoring the noon whistle. At exactly 1200, 25 August A.D. 1944, we cranked up and rolled across the Seine at Pont de Sèvres. But for occasional out-of-bounds rounds plunked into the rollicking scenery by the German batteries at the Longchamps course, there' was nothing to remind us that the advance was a military action and not a pictorial parade into pandemonium.

"You Were There," the TV program which tried to reconstruct historical events, some years ago dramatized the loony liberation. It signally failed to recapture anything even vaguely familiar. Mass delirium and military moonshine, while rapturous to the participant, are much too elusive for art.

Scouts and heralds, with trumpets and dodgers, must have been sent forward to muster the crowd. For Paris was already alerted to the entry and had cast off its chains, though the Germans formally still held the city. For the first mile or so of march, there was repeated the wild, high carnival of the prior afternoon, except that the crush had thickened and was less controllable. In our jeep we gulped and we wept. Elena had lofted the American flag and the sight of that banner, more than all else, stirred the beholders to the highest pitch of ecstasy. Again, the mothers came running with babies to be kissed, the aging ex-*poilus* stood at salute, the little boys screamed for cigarettes and the champagne donors rushed the vehicles. But the Paris mob was a little different, better prepared, more sophisticated. Skirts were shorter and hair-dos more conspicuous. Half the women carried flowers to be tossed or bright bunting to be strewn over the vehicles. Platoons of photographers and autograph hunters pressed in close. Caught up in the excitement, everyone aboard the column would have been content that things stay this way right to the end.

Place-St.-Cloud is the first roundabout beyond the Sèvres bridge. As the jeep turned into its spacious circle, suddenly the column blocked solid. We could not see why. The clamor had ceased. The central garden of the circle was utterly deserted as was its outer rim, which is built up solid with apartment houses. That one moment was pregnant with silence, made more awesome because there was no explaining it.

Then two things happened right together. A volley of rifle fire erupted directly behind us and an artillery shell out of nowhere struck and felled a chestnut tree on the parkway so that it fell as a screen between the jeep and the nearest apartment building, thirty yards to our right. In those few seconds while the tree was settling, the tanks and cars ahead of us became emptied of their people (including Hemingway) as they ran for the buildings on the far side of the circle, such was the effect of the surprise fire. We couldn't follow the stampede. All of the rifle fire was coming from the building just back of the jeep and the fallen tree. Westover crawled to one end of the tree so that he could cover the windows with his carbine. Elena stayed in the center. My part of it was to watch the other end lest someone from the lower story (which we couldn't see because of the tree) tried to push through the foliage toward us.

Punctuated by random rifle fire, this interlude lasted not more than five minutes. Then there was a roar and rattle from the direction we had come. Six French halftracks followed by five tanks raced into the circle, turned inside the stalled column, and continued round and round the circle with their machine guns wide open, blazing at the building we were facing. That fire grazed just above the jeep and stripped every twig and leaf from the upper part of the fallen tree. During the ten or so minutes that the French armor played merry-go-round, honoring our sector as if it only contained the brass ring, not less than 5000 bullets zipped directly above our heads or buzzed past our bottoms. It was not a choice spot to be stranded. There was nothing to do but hug the gutter and curb. Westover sang, "I'll See You Again," through his teeth, which was always his habit when the wind was slightly up, a sign that he was thinking of home and Eloise. The Spanish girl said: "*Tengo mieda mucho,*" and laughed like hell to prove it. She was worth any ten duchesses in such moments. We knew great fear and high excitement exquisitely mixed, for it was touch-and-go whether we'd come out. The shooting stopped when there was nothing left to fire. We were whole-skinned and not yet shaking. The whole thing was stark mad and the escape of our party was due to pure luck and not to the quality of French marksmanship. We had heard any number of bullets zing as they bounced off pavement and curb. Still, the jeep was untouched.

The tanks pulled off. The place quieted. We heard a man yelling from a great distance. Then we saw him and the sight was more whimsical than all else. He was on the third-floor balcony of the apartment building across the circle and he was hunched far over as he scuttled along. "Looks like Lon Chaney haunting Notre Dame," said Westover. The man had his hands cupped and though he shouted in French the words barely cut through the wind. But we knew the voice. It was Papa again.

"What's he saying?" This to Elena.

She answered: "There are Germans in the building behind us. We have to get out. The French are bringing in artillery to blow the place down."

We got out. Elena went first, taking those eighty yards like a startled doe; we following at 20-second intervals, with Westover coming last so that he could cover the windows against snipers during the getaway. Not one hostile round dignified the extrication. When we made the portal on the far side, there was Papa with his carbine at shoulder, laying down the covering barrage. That was a big building and he could hardly have missed it. The French artillery duly arrived and did its sterling stuff. Whether there were ever any Germans in the apartment or the fire had come from a few rascals trying to make whoopee was never proved to the satisfaction of the trio closest to the scene. In any case, if the situation was as painted, it would have been better handled by a half-squad armed with a dozen hand grenades. But that would have been poor theater.

Soon after the column had its last hurrah at the head of Avenue Foch, we said goodbye to Elena. A French major came down the line screaming: "Get these _____ women out of the vehicles." That had to be resisted, since the honor of a very gentle person was concerned. So the major was told off, loudly, profanely. From behind me, a voice roared: "You tell 'em, Marshall. Since when hasn't a soldier the right to company in his sleeping bag? That's the way I won _____," but the name was lost in the roar of approval from the crowd. Papa's wisecrack got to her, where the major had failed. Without a word she slipped away to seek her lover and we never saw her again.

From the Étoile, John and I drove on the short run to Hôtel Claridge. We were tired. The desk clerk refused us a room though the hotel clearly was untenanted. We demanded to see the manager, and when he came forth, our money was on the counter.

He said: "There are no rooms. This hotel is reserved for the German Army."

I said: "You've got just five seconds to get it unreserved. This is the American Army moving in." We got the rooms and quickly learned the reason for the attempted stall. Each bathroom bore a neat sign bidding warm welcome to German officers. The embarrassed host wanted time to remove them.

The story was told at the clambake in the Ritz that night, which put it in circulation. Jack Ritz commented drolly: "What could you expect? Hotel men have no country. They're the only true internationalists." Here is the probable basis of the greatly embroidered legend about Hemingway's liberating the Ritz. Wrong hotel. Wrong cast. I know Jack was waiting there with Dunhill pipes as souvenirs for each of us when we made the Ritz lobby, slightly ahead of Papa.

Until the last dog was left unhung, the grand event had these overtones of opera bouffe. Von Cholitz, the enemy commander, had his headquarters in Hôtel Meurice, that monument to the rococo. In early evening a tank went by the Meurice, fired one round at an ancient Chevy parked alongside and set it afire. That was enough boom-boom to save Von Cholitz's honor. He and twenty of his staff officers came running from the hotel, hands in air. Von Cholitz, with his boys stringing along, was taken to Montparnasse where Leclerc told him to surrender the twenty spots where Germans still held out. Captain Paul Sapiebra, USA, wrote out twenty copies of a surrender order and Von Cholitz signed them. The twenty staff officers were then loaded in twenty jeeps and speeded to twenty points of resistance. That no more ended the sniping than did the next morning's sun tranquilize the throb of the hangover. But it was the formal ending to the German occupation and the story.

INDEX